Introduction

Welcome to *Memories of Chester,* a look back on the city through a series of lovely old photographs, chosen according to their ability to rekindle memories of the past. In selecting the pictures the emphasis has been on scenes and events from the 1940s, '50s and '60s. Scenes which should be within the memory of many readers - this is not a book about Roman relics, or even bowler hats and crinolines! Neither is *Memories of Chester* a book about local history in the normal sense; it has far more to do with entertainment than serious study, though I hope you will agree it is none the worse for that. It is hoped that the images on the following pages will prompt memories of the *Chester* known by readers in days gone-by. We are always pleased to receive letters from people who can add to the information which accompanies the pictures so that it may be included in future reprints.

Many local companies have allowed us to study their archives to recount their history in the book - and fascinating reading it makes too. The present-day guardians of the firms concerned are proud of their products and the achievements of their people. We are pleased to be able to provide them with a platform through which they can share their story with a wider audience.

When I began compiling *Memories of Chester* several months ago I anticipated that the task would be a pleasurable one, but my expectations have been greatly surpassed. The quality of the photographs I have been privileged to use has been superb, and the assistance I have received from the staff of Chester's Reference Library and the *Chester Chronicle* has made my work very enjoyable.

Chester has been the subject of many royal visits over the years and several of them are featured in the book. Civic and military processions are included too, and hundreds of Chester people can be seen lining the streets on these occasions and looking on from every vantage point. Perhaps you might see yourself or a relative on one of the photographs?

Street scenes are well covered, and the photographs are brought to life by a variety of delightful old motor vehicles. Some of my favourite pictures are those featuring busy shoppers going about their daily business, unaware of the photographer recording the scene for us to see today.

Memories of Chester has been a pleasure to compile, I hope you enjoy reading it.
Happy memories!

Phil Holland
True North Books

First published in Great Britain by True North Books
Dean Clough
Halifax HX3 5AX
1997

© TRUE NORTH HOLDINGS
ISBN 1 900 463 46 6

Contents

Right: A picture taken in 1953 of Lowe and Sons who dealt in gold, antique silver and Sheffield plate. To celebrate the Coronation of Queen Elizabeth II they sported window boxes of red, white and blue flowers. A large Union Jack flies between the upper windows and smaller flags are tucked behind wall shields decorated with more Union Jacks.

Events

The honouring of the Cheshire Regiment by the City of Chester in September 1948 involved granting them permission to march though the streets with bayonets fixed. We see them here as they pass the decorated Town Hall steps and saluting dais erected in front of the Town Hall. Military music was provided on the day by the band of the Cheshire Regiment. Over 200 officers and men from the 1st Battalion The Cheshire Regiment took part in the parade, commanded by Major F. J Gold, along with the 7th Battalion of the Cheshire Territorial Army and representatives of the Old Comrades Association and Cheshire County Army Cadets. The Colonel of the Regiment Colonel G.P Harding C.B.E, D.S.O, M.S.O took the salute alongside the Mayor of Chester and was presented with a silver casket and illuminated vellum scroll in a ceremony afterwards. Every possible vantage point had been taken - every window sill, rooftop and balcony, as the proud folk of Chester looked on at the impressive, historic spectacle.

Right: The rather chilly and damp weather could not prevent huge crowds lining the streets of Chester in October 1949 when Her Majesty Queen Elizabeth - later the Queen Mother - visited Chester. The royal motorcade is seen here passing through Eastgate, beneath the clock which had been positioned there 52 years earlier to celebrate Queen Victoria's Jubilee. The Royal Train had arrived at the General Station at 10.30 am from Balmoral. Princess Margaret was with her mother but she remained on the train while her mother went into Chester to fulfil her engagements. Throughout the visit the Queen was accompanied by the Mayor of Chester and the Mayoress Mr and Mrs Bert Reynolds, along with the Viscount and Viscountess Leverhulme. The main purpose of the visit was to inspect the officers and men of the Queen's Bays Regiment at the Dale, Upton-by-Chester. During the ceremony it rained quite heavily but the participants and onlookers refused to let this spoil the occasion. On returning to the railway station Her Majesty was presented with a posy of flowers by the Mayor's granddaughter, 4 year-old Jacqueline Reynolds. As she boarded the Royal Train the Queen paused with the Mayor and said "I think Chester is a lovely old City. I am delighted at the great welcome they gave me today - and I am particularly delighted that so many school children were present. The City's loyalty has touched me deeply."

Below: Thousands of people gathered to honour the brave men of the Cheshire Regiment in the centre of Chester in September 1948. It was not only the men and women who had some connection with the Regiment who turned out to honour the soldiers - it seemed as if the whole town had gathered to see them. The ceremony took place on the Town Hall Square, in front of the canopied-steps of the Town Hall. The troops were inspected by the Mayor, Councillor Robert Frost and the Regimental Colours were 'cased' for the Parade as can be seen in this picture.

The celebrations which took place as a result of the coronation of Her Majesty Queen Elizabeth II in 1953 were extensive in Chester. The fact that the Queen and the Duke of Edinburgh had visited the area quite recently probably helped to generate additional interest. This picture shows the elaborate decorations at Eastgate. The area was awash with a sea of colour in the days leading up to the coronation. Sir Hugh Casson was commissioned by *Browns* to decorate the outside of the famous store. Browns generously gave their staff a bonus of one-month's additional pay and the day off as part of the coronation celebrations. It became a talking point in the city as it was well known that Hugh Casson was in charge of the decorations for the coronation in Westminster. Along Eastgate there were large pictures of the past queens of England hanging on the walls.

Continued overleaf

Across the gates of the city crimson drapes were hung with gold decorations to give them a 'regal' appearance. A banner was displayed at the General Station proclaiming "God grant her a record run!"

The Tatler Cinema organised the showing of the event on a large screen TV. This was very advanced for the time, the image being shown on a 9ft by 7ft screen as opposed to the actual cinema screen itself. Over 100 tickets were sold at the not inconsiderable price of 25 shillings each. For this the guests received a pre-packed lunch (supplied by the Plane Tree Cafe) plus tea and coffee throughout the day - along with the services of attendants who would run errands for the guests during the seven- hour broadcast. Of course, the whole of Chester joined in celebrations on the day, with scores of organised street-parties throughout the area providing memories for everyone to look back on.

Right: A shower of rain was doing its best to put the damper on the 1957 Royal visit, but everyone present on the day agreed that it had failed to spoil the occasion. The unsung hero in this picture was Mr. Mansell Aston of the Clerks Department of the County Council. His skillful use of the umbrella gained the appreciation of Her Majesty as they left the County Hall.

Construction work on the County Hall had begun in 1938 but the war interrupted the job and it served as an air-raid precaution centre until the end of the conflict. For many years the building existed as a stark one-storey shell. One purpose of the Queen's 1957 visit was to formally open the building. Inside she was presented to Lilian Bromley-Davenport the Vice Chairman of the County Council and Dr. G.A. Ellison, the Bishop of Chester. Her Majesty was presented with a silver cigarette case which carried a picture of her favourite racehorse. It had been supplied by Lowe and Sons of Bridge Street Row. Members of the County Council were assembled in the new Council chamber to witness the presentation and the unveiling of a plaque by Her Majesty.

The warmth of the Chester welcome given to Her Majesty the Queen and the Duke of Edinburgh on their visit in 1957 is evident here. The royal couple are seen leaving the Infirmary in this photograph, the extent of the security presence seems to be limited to this hospital porter and his outstretched arms. A far cry from the precautions necessary in modern times. The picture shows the Matron, Miss E. Brown walking beside the Queen, with Mr G.B Elphick, the deputy chairman of the Hospital Management Committee, bringing up the rear. Light rain was beginning to fall as the royal party left the Infirmary - but that doesn't seem to have dampened the enthusiasm of these loyal subjects. At the end of the visit Miss Brown told reporters how the Queen had asked her about the staff in the Infirmary, and what all the different coloured uniforms meant. She described how the Queen had been friendly and 'natural' throughout the visit and managed to put everyone at ease when they met her.

Right: This military ceremony was part of the programme of events at a royal visit to Chester in May 1957. The venue was Eaton Hall and the picture was taken in May 1957. The picture shows Her Royal Highness the Princess Royal receiving the ceremonial belt from Senior Under Officer I.M.R. Smart. The Princess Royal had been visiting the area to take the salute at the Passing Out Parade at Eaton Hall. Pictured with the Princess Royal and I.M.R. Smart is the Commandant, B.O.P. Eugster.

Bottom and far right: A youthful and beautiful Queen Elizabeth II is seen here in the Childrens' ward of Chester's Royal Infirmary. Her visit was part of the itinerary created for Her Majesty and the Duke of Edinburgh when they came to the city in July 1957. The little lads seem rather more interested in having their picture taken than paying attention to the monarch. This could not be said about the nursing sister in the background - no doubt this encounter would be the highlight of her nursing career. We know from contemporary descriptions that Her Majesty was wearing a powder-blue fitted coat of corded-silk, a ruched silk hat in darker blue, and three-quarter length white gloves. The outfit was completed by contrasting blue shoes and a matching handbag. The Queen received a rousing welcome as the royal limousines drew up outside the Infirmary. Girls from the Queen's School had cheered along Nuns Road chanting "Vivat Regina!" Crowds had been gathering there since 8.00 am and no one complained about the light rain which showered down intermittently. During the visit to the Infirmary the Queen signed the visitors' book and presented two signed photographs featuring herself and the Duke of Edinburgh to be displayed in the Outpatients Department.

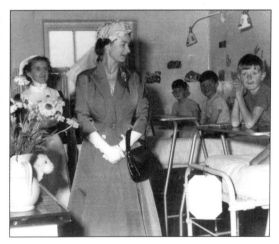

Extensive redecoration took place along Eastgate Street in 1966. This photograph records the official opening of the street after the work had been completed. In the foreground, towards the centre of the picture, Lord Kennet can be seen, looking upwards at some of the fine detail on one of the buildings, and shading his eyes from the summer sunshine. On the far right Chester's best-known clock is in view, sitting above the Eastgate as it had done since 1897. "The Eastgate" originally led into Eastgate Street. Now there is only the arch it once filled. Many of the buildings here show early examples of the Chester black-and-white revival. Early in the nineteenth century the street was a mixture of genuine but dilapidated half-timbered structures and newer Georgian brick. There followed a mid-nineteenth century battle of styles in the street, the outcome of which is a surprisingly satisfying blend of contrasting properties. A month before this picture was taken Chester had been in the news with a terrible story that had made the headlines all around the world. At Chester Assizes Ian Brady, 28, and Myra Hindley, 23 were both sentenced to life imprisonment at the "Bodies on the Moors" trial after being found guilty of murder.

CAPITAL BANK - a remarkable Chester success story

The origins of the business which grew into Chester's largest employer can be traced back to a Morris motor dealership which had its head office in Colwyn Bay. The *Braid Group* had several other garages selling Vauxhall cars and had set up *Improved Finance Limited* in 1945 in order to provide loans on the vehicles purchased from them. Initially, during the first few years after the war, trade remained at a modest level as the economy struggled to get back on its feet. As consumer confidence

returned in post-war Britain some far-sighted operators in the finance industry predicted that consumer spending would soon show considerable increases. A consequence of this would be rapid growth in demand for loans on all kinds of domestic and industrial products.

Scenes from the sixties:
*Above: Girls in the accounts department. **Right:** The collection department. **Far Right:** The tiny offices at 19 Newgate Street, Chester.*

A milestone in the development of the organisation was passed in 1948 when the decision was made to sell financial services through other motor dealerships in the north west. It was decided that a change of name would help attract more business, as would a move away from Colwyn Bay in order to get physically closer to the clients it intended to serve. By December 1948 the business had moved into the tiny offices at 19 Newgate Street and began trading as *North West Securities*. The move to Chester almost didn't happen. The first general manager, Sydney Jones wanted to base the business in Liverpool rather than Chester because he favoured working in big cities. Robert Braid, the Chairman, disagreed, on the principle that the company could attract 'Liverpool' business into Chester but not vice versa. In later years, looking back on the conversation, Sydney Jones happily agreed that the move to Chester was the right decision and that it was an important element in the early success of the company.

around this time that a relationship was established with an insurance broker in Coventry. Leads were fed back to the Chester office marking the company's first steps towards a geographical expansion.

It had taken a long time, but post-war confidence was having a positive effect on the demand for loans and credit by the 1950s. Better living standards and ever-increasing aspirations brought additional business and further growth. By 1954 the Liverpool branch had opened and Sydney Jones began to build a management team capable of taking the company on to even greater heights. During the 1950s the provision of loans to industry was a growing part of North West Securities' business. The contribution made by Sydney Jones was recognised in 1955 when he was appointed a director. The following year Norwest House was built in Newgate Street, Chester. It became the new Head Office.

The staff in those early days consisted of Sydney Jones and just two ladies providing administrative support. Early records show that the first advance made by North West Securities was for a Vauxhall 10 saloon, registration mark KNW 948, costing £607.18. At this time relationships were developing with motor dealers throughout the region who would contact the office with applications for motor loans on behalf of their customers. Early seeds were planted in other industries and soon loans were being made for the purchase of industrial plant, machinery and buildings. Later, existing domestic clients were encouraged to contact the company when they needed loans for other purposes, and the business flourished. It was

Above: Left to right: Mr E. R. Hazlehurst, Mr S. A. Jones and Mr R. A. Allen.
Right: Norwest House, the company's headquarters from 1956 to 1963.

In 1957 the Preston branch was opened as new business for that year exceeded the £1m milestone for the first time. Much of this growth related to the increasing proportion of car sales which were funded by hire purchase - up from 7% of all new car sales in 1950 to 21% in 1957. It is, perhaps, surprising these days to consider that strict controls were applied by the government in the years after the war on the terms and conditions of hire purchase agreements. Towards the end of the decade the Chancellor of the Exchequer announced the relaxation of controls on finance. Within weeks many major banks had acquired a holding in the larger finance houses. It was against this background that, early in August 1958, a sub-committee of Bank of Scotland, chaired by Lord Bilsland the Governor, met to decide whether to buy a stake in a large, publicly-quoted company, or to consider the outright purchase of one of the smaller independent companies in this developing field. Bank of Scotland was a respected player in the

Banking field with a history going back as far as 1695. The organisation had been through a period of reorganisation and enlargement during the 1950s in response to the difficult conditions which prevailed at the end of the Second War and the threat of nationalisation and lending restrictions which characterised the era and made bankers anxious. By the end of August 1958 Bank of Scotland had decided to enter negotiations with the *Braid Motor Group* with a view to purchasing North West Securities. Tough discussions took place at the Adelphi Hotel in Liverpool and eventually a price was agreed upon. The following years saw considerable investment by Bank of Scotland and the establishment of a large network of NWS branches across the U.K, coinciding with a boom in personal expenditure which had obvious benefits for the company. Total hire-purchase debt in the U.K had almost doubled between 1958 and 1960 and NWS succeeded in gaining a healthy share of this growth.

The growth of the value of the organisation's assets in the years after Bank of Scotland became involved

Left: NWS House in City Road completed in 1962. Above: The Mayor of Chester, Councillor T. Sarl Williams, visiting the typing pool following the official opening of NWS House in June 1963.

in the organisation allowed a series of takeovers which characterised the company's development over the next four decades. The first of these was the acquisition of *Harcoden Finance* in 1960. Additional branches were opened at Leeds, Bristol and the City of London in 1963, bringing the total up to 23. These branches were small and concentrated upon using the specialist knowledge of the staff there to attract new business. Accounting and administrative functions were conducted at Head Office. Another milestone was passed during the 1960s when the number of clients 'on the books' passed the 30,000 mark. During this decade growth was achieved in the area of industrial and agricultural loans and finance for businesses large and small, built upon a reputation for being 'friendly people to deal with.'

The growth in the firm's activities and continued prosperity meant that it was desirable and possible to create new premises in which to conduct these enhanced levels of business. NWS House was constructed on a site adjacent to the Queen Hotel in City Road as an eight storey block. It was opened in June 1963 by the Mayor Of Chester Councillor T. Sarl-Williams. Prior to the opening of the new accommodation it had been necessary for the company to

spread its workload across five different offices in the city. The new block was the largest commercial building in Chester when it opened .

Much of the company's success had been achieved by employing talented people and giving them the 'room and responsibility' to manage their operations. Between 1964 and 1968 pre-tax profit rose from just over £402,000 to £1 million - a remarkable achievement.

By 1971 North West Securities had 56 branches across England, Scotland, Wales and Northern Ireland. Personal finance was offered on a wide range of products including cars, caravans, boats, sports and hobby equipment, home extensions, renovations, furnishings and domestic appliances. A range of normal banking facilities was in place as well as the company's unique *Paymaster Plan* which offered an innovative and extremely flexible way of financing medium-priced

items such as clothing, holidays, and gardening. Commercial clients were attracted to the leasing and finance facilities for a broad range of market and product sectors. The variety and scope of the business

Left: Girls enjoying the rooftop view from the top of NWS House. **Above:** *The spacious accounts department as it appeared in the mid 1960s.*

grew, and finance for aircraft, fishing and other vessels, railway wagons and commercial and industrial plant of all kinds.

1971 also saw North West Securities create the Industrial Bank of Scotland Ltd., and by the end of the year it was able to offer full banking facilities in Inverness, Edinburgh and Glasgow under the In-Bank brand. This was another period of tremendous growth and success for the organisation. Profits for 1972 were almost double those achieved just three years earlier, a truly breathtaking performance.

The mid 1970s saw alliances being formed with manufacturers in key industries for the provision of finance. One of the most successful of these was formed with Renault UK to provide loans and credit facilities on Renault cars and vans. Most importantly, it paved the way for similar arrangements with other motor manufacturers, and the subsequent opportunity to reach even greater numbers of private finance clients. A further important development in the 1970s was the launch of the North West Securities Budget Accounts operation. This coincided with what was described as a revolution in high street shopping when major stores began to offer credit cards for regular customers. Two major forces on the high street, Marks & Spencer and C & A, both launched schemes in conjunction with NWS. The additional activity undertaken in these areas led to further increases in pre-tax profits, up to £8.3 million in 1978, more than

six times greater than those recorded ten years earlier. Sydney Jones retired in 1979 after 31 years with the company, being replaced by Ray Hazlehurst. Sydney and his staff had achieved a remarkable feat. It had been 21 years since North West Securities had been acquired by Bank of Scotland and the company had risen from 155th in the rankings of the Finance Houses Association to 5th.

North West Securities was quick to see the possibilities afforded by the increasingly sophisticated market techniques associated with Direct Mail. Throughout the '80s additional business was secured through this medium and the new strategy enabled the company to bring an increasing range of financial services to the attention of the people most likely to require them. The organisation's innovative approach in this field was recognised by the British Direct Mail Association when they awarded NWS the Gold Medal in the finance category.

By 1982 there were 68 branches throughout Britain and continued development enabled the company to attract an enviable list of blue chip clients.

1984 saw the launch of two important initiatives. *Capital Vehicle Contracts Limited* was created to provide hire facilities for business vehicles. Agreement was reached during the same year to takeover the administration of the Boots Charge Card - a considerable undertaking covering Boots' 1200 stores throughout the country, and the provision of a personal loans facility to holders of the Boots Charge Card. Success here was followed by one of the most important developments in the history of NWS. The launch of the Automobile Association's AA Visa Card was followed by the AA Budget Account and, the following year the launch of AA Financial Services. This enabled NWS to offer a wide range of financial services to the association's 6,000,000 members. Ultimately the skills and experience gained during this period would pave the way for similar alliances

Above: The reception of NWS House in 1962

of *The Mortgage Business plc* heralded a move into another market sector - the provision of domestic home mortgages. Such was the progress here that by 1994 the operation was voted 'best for quality of service, efficiency and competitiveness' after a survey of leading mortgage providers by Commercial Union.

Further progress was made in the 1990s with the acquisition of Equity Bank of Dublin. Reorganisation and restructuring resulted in major improvements in efficiency and profitability which have positioned the Irish arm of the organisation's activities at the forefront of Irish banking activities. Other recent developments include the launch of NFU Mutual Finance, a joint company with the NFU Mutual Insurance, which provides finance for the farming community.

John Mercer, the current managing director appointed in 1994, has continued with an investment programme to ensure that the company retains its position as one of the UK's leading finance houses.

1997 saw a change of name to CAPITAL BANK, a decision based on the need to project an image which reflects the increased breadth of business activities now undertaken. The business has developed, through shrewd management and an innovative approach to creating highly satisfied clients, from arranging finance for that first Vauxhall saloon to a position where enquiries for loans to purchase oil rigs and airliners are handled almost routinely. The company is proud of the achievements of the people who have made CAPITAL BANK the respected financial institution it is today.... and pleased that it chose Chester as the hub of its operations around half a century ago.

Above left: Capital House, CAPITAL BANK'S centre for its direct telemarketing operation.

which would play a significant part in the company's future strategy and success.

The appointment of Mr. Harry Bush as managing director in 1986 was also the start of a period of reorganisation, restructuring and further exceptional growth. A series of partnerships were established with a number of leading building societies. The 1980s are also remembered for a series of ambitious building projects designed to create state-of-the-art accommodation for the expanding Chester workforce. The

chosen site was on City Road, behind NWS House and in 1987 the first new building, Computer House, was completed and occupied by the Management Services Division. The following year Capital House was completed nearby and occupied by the company's direct telesales operation.

The end of the decade witnessed another important change to the status of the company as banking status was conferred upon it. This resulted in a change of name - to *NWS BANK plc.* Soon afterwards the launch

Around the city centre

Below: This picture is over 60 years old and features the familiar, yet subtly-different view up St. Werburgs Street as it appeared in the 1930s. The impressive building on the left was occupied by Parr's Bank at the time the picture was taken - it is better known to its modern customers as the National Westminster Bank of course. Above the bank were offices from where the Legal Insurance Company conducted its business in Chester. The Bank of Liverpool (est. 1831) was situated in the right of the picture from the premises later to be taken over by Martin's Bank. Other businesses shown include the Tamil Cafe and The Rubber Shop. There were no traffic lights, but the point-duty police officer complete with white coat for driver-visibility is present to control the flow of traffic. The north side of the street is dominated by the Cathedral in this picture. Until the nineteenth century this was a narrow lane. Timber framed buildings on the east side were designed by John Douglas and the ornamental detail includes oriel windows carved figures and 'barley sugar' chimneys. A modern range of shops opposite the Cathedral has provided Chester with a further example of the covered footpaths for which she has become so well known.

Above: The Cathedral dominates this photograph of St. Werburgs Street which was taken in the 1930s. Signs for many of the small businesses which occupied the street at the time can be clearly seen. Examples include the Tamil Cafe, The Rubber Shop, Lush and Cook Ltd., the dyers and cleaners, Millicents the florists and Mackworth's, the civil and military tailors. On the left of the picture, the entrance to the branch of a rather larger business, the Norwich Union, is just visible. On the right of the picture a bus stop can be seen. It seems hard to imagine that there was ever room for queues of people and 'bus traffic on this street - but somehow they seemed to manage. The curious lady on the right of the picture is standing at an arch which has, for some reason been removed, near the entrance to Martins Bank.

Below: A picture dating from around 1925 which features the Eastgate of Chester and the distinctive clock positioned above it. The clock was sited here as part of the celebrations marking the Jubilee of Queen Victoria, a gift to the people of Chester which has become one of the most photographed objects in the city. The large white building on the right of the street is, of course, the Burtons building, the location of the Chester branch of this well known and successful gents outfitters. Stewart King the tailor was located in the 'traditional' black and white building next door to Burtons, and the lovely old W.H Smith booksellers and stationers' property is nearest to the camera.

Above: 1930s Eastgate Street and the Eastgate is pictured here. Uncharacteristically, the street seems rather quiet from the point of view of traffic levels, and this is probably a deliberate attempt by the photographer to choose a moment when the scene was not dominated by motorcars. The premises of the National Westminster Bank can be seen on the left of the picture, though at this time the bank was under the ownership of *Parrs*. The people of Chester cannot fail to be proud of their City when they look at street scenes like this one. Much of the distinctiveness of Chester is contained within the walls of the city. Many visitors are surprised to learn that the 'black and white revival' which has generated such character on the streets of Chester only dates from the 1850s and continued well into the present century. In relatively recent times attempts have been made to reduce the amount of traffic flowing through the centre of Chester and create shopping areas which are safer and more pleasant for people visiting the centre. The ring road has been successful in separating 'local' and through 'traffic' - previously a huge headache both for local people trying to go about their business, and for travellers trying to reach the towns and cities beyond.

The Rows are a unique survival from the Middle Ages and were formerly more extensive in Chester. Several of the shops at street level incorporate medieval cellars or crypts. There are Rows on both sides of Bridge Street. On the east side they are high, wide and light and are used as a modern shopping arcade. It runs continuously from the Heritage Centre to the Cross. On the west side it begins suddenly as an entrance to the first floor of Owen Owens, the department store, and is broken by the need to cross Commonhall Street. It contains few shop entrances and is less used than the Row opposite. In Hemingway's time, the east side was mainly occupied by butchers and, on market days the middle of the road was continually blocked by coal merchants' carts. This picture taken at the Cross in Bridge Street, at the junction with Eastgate Street, dates from the thirties. Shop proprietors then included Hudson Verity, S Fielden and B Walton. There was a shop selling artists' materials here and a jeweller. In the centre foreground is a news vendor with papers under his arm. A lady wheels an uncomfortable-looking baby's pram and a youth of fifteen or so wears short trousers.

This lovely old view of the centre of Chester may be rather on the *old side* to rekindle the memories of most local people. The exact date it was taken is uncertain, though the vehicles in the picture suggest it may have been in the 1920s or '30s. One clue is the fact that tramlines are still visible in the road, sweeping away from the camera. Eastgate row and *Boots* the chemist is visible on the right of the picture in the block containing *Gerry's High Class Dispensing Pharmacy.* We wonder whether Gerry's was *high-class* enough to resist the stiff competition from his powerful neighbour!

In the distance, almost in the centre of the picture, we can see the property occupied by the *Etonian,* a substantial tailoring and gents' outfitting firm of the day. The property at the corner, on the right of the picture, is one of the most distinctive and recognisable pieces of architecture in Chester. It was extensively rebuilt in 1888.

A fine old photograph from 1948. The Eastgate and the ornamental clock just visible above it dominates the scene which is given an additional feeling of nostalgia by the curvaceous motorcars in the foreground. The white facade of the Burtons building can be seen peeping over the Eastgate on the left of the picture. A sign directing people to the King's Arms Kitchen can be seen on the left wall of the Eastgate, with *Huxleys* opposite. A John Lewis delivery van is visible through the archway. 1948 is remembered as the year which saw the nationalisation of British railways in January and the electricity industry in April. In America the nation mourned the passing of the US aviator Orville Wright and in Europe the first seeds which grew into the *Common Market* were sown.

The north side of Eastgate Street and the Eastgate is featured in this picture from 1951. There are two branches of Woolworths in the photograph and other businesses include Mac Fisheries, Kardomah and B. Walton and Son the Jewellers. Martins Bank is just in view on the left. Eastgate Street was long considered the principal street in Chester. Hundreds of relics from Roman times have been found in this area over the years - the majority of which have ended up in the Grosvenor Museum. Considering the importance of Eastgate Street, it is not surprising that the Eastgate was the main entrance and exit to Chester. The archway we know today dates from 1769 (remarkably, 20 years before the French Revolution) and it replaced a medieval structure which was narrow, for defensive reasons and flanked by octagonal towers.

A view along Bridge Street from the junction with Grosvenor Street, with the familiar outline of St. Peter's Church in the distance. St. Peter's was built close to where four main streets met, in the middle of the City. It is often said that the architecture of St. Peter's is outclassed by its richer history. That is a matter of opinion, but it is a fact that various stages of rebuilding have obscured many interesting medieval features within the structure. Note that the spire still graced the tower of the church in this 1950s scene. It was later removed. The High Cross was restored to its position south of the church porch in 1975. The plan of the church is considered unusual because it has no nave or chancel. Three arcades divide the church into four aisles, so in plain view it appears to be almost square. The churchyard was used for burials until the opening of Chester Cemetery (south of the river) in the middle of the last century. In modern times it is now a quiet, paved area within the precincts of the church.

This picture was taken in 1948. The shops here are, from the left, Marstons, selling Raleigh Cycles, Willerbys Tailors and the English Leather Company. Then come H. Jeffersons, Drapery and Hosiery, Shaws the Ironmongers. Siddalls, established 1815 and on the right of the picture, was an 'Optician and Umbrella-Maker.'

> "ST. PETER'S CHURCH WAS BUILT CLOSE TO WHERE FOUR MAIN STREETS MET, IN THE MIDDLE OF THE CITY."

The dampness in this day creates an atmospheric scene in this photograph. It dates from 1951 and features the south side of Eastgate street. This was the area, along with Foregate, which was targeted by the big national retail chains as they grew and expanded into the regions during the 1920s and 1930s. Many, though not all of the small businesses which had occupied these streets were displaced as the major stores moved in. It was a similar story in many other towns throughout the country as the world of shopping became increasingly dominated by the massive national chains and their huge resources. An assortment of vehicles is shown in this picture, just in view, on the left, is a flat-backed lorry making deliveries to licensed premises in the City. On the news front, 1951 was the year that Winston Churchill was returned again as Prime Minister in the October General Election, and the Festival of Britain Gardens were opened in Battersea.

Foregate Street follows the line of the main Roman Road out of Chester and takes its name from its position "before" or outside the Eastgate. Since the 1960s the east end has witnessed a complex system of traffic movement. At the west end it has developed into a very busy shopping area as a consequence of the congregation of several chain stores at the location. The picture was taken in the summer of 1948 and it is interesting to note that all the older ladies in the view, and some of the younger ones, are wearing hats.

Above: This scene showing Foregate was captured from the city wall. It was originally taken for use on a greetings card and so has probably had widespread circulation over the years. The Blossoms Hotel is featured - in 1856 it was described as "a house of the highest standing and respectability." In those days it had a very different appearance, being brick-built in Georgian style. It was rebuilt on the same site in 1896 with the upper storeys half-timbered in true Chester fashion. This photograph was taken in the 1950s and features Belisha-Beacons to mark the position of pedestrian crossings. These early attempts at improving the safety of pedestrians were named after the Minister of Transport at the time of the 1930 Road Traffic Act - Mr. Hore- Belisha.

Below: 'Round the back' of Browns of Chester. The picture shows work being done on the 5th September 1964. The workmen have not been issued with overalls but wear their own 'uniform' of rolled up shirt sleeves, sleeveless pullovers and cloth cap. Browns is one of only three shops in Chester whose original crypt has been neither destroyed nor drastically altered.

Above: The imposing gabled building housing the Coach and Horses public house at the top of Princess Street is featured here. Until the early nineteenth century Princess Street was *Parson's Lane*, where the vicar of St. Oswald's church had a house. Later came terraced houses, and, by the 1930s the whole area behind the Town Hall and old market hall as far as Trinity Street had become a notorious slum area. Of course, in modern times the street shows no signs of that part of its past. The photograph dates from July 1959 and shows a bus driver in full uniform striding across the street. There was obviously no *turning a blind eye* or concessions to the heat of the summer in those days! A queue of people can be seen at the bus shelter on the right of the picture. Of course, bus shelters and other public facilities were unlikely to be the targets of vandalism that they tend to be these days. Indeed, 'vandalism' at that time was not an everyday expression.

Below: A picture taken in Crane Street in 1966. The Watergate of the Middle Ages stood not far from the edge of the River Dee. It was the principal entrance for goods unloaded from the wharves. After the river was canalised in 1730, new wharves were built and New Crane Street was constructed to link them to Watergate. It is now a main route west from the city centre, leading to the modern trading estate at Sealand Road. Till the 1960s it contained a major bottleneck because of the swing bridge over the spur that connected the Shropshire Canal with the Dee. The bad condition of the fencing round the wasteland here has allowed easy access for gypsy caravans, much to the consternation of some residents in the city.

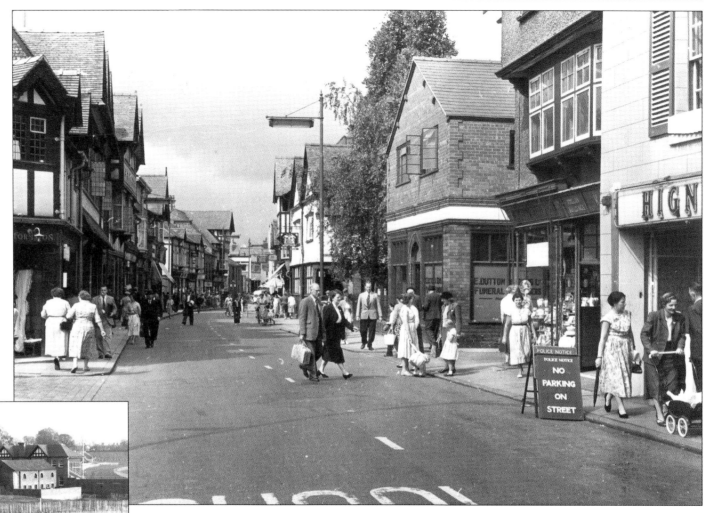

Above: This view of Frodsham Street demonstrates just how different it was in scale and appearance from Foregate Street. The former rustic name of the street was Cow Lane, though this belies its importance as one of the main roads into Chester. Before the construction of the inner ring road it bore most of the traffic to and from Warrington and the north. The street was once described as "narrow, filthy and inconvenient." Much of this area was rebuilt in the nineteenth century. In more recent times the 1969 Insall Report described the location as "a largely undistinguished and disjointed street scene" - so that bad press has continued well into the twentieth century! In this picture several pedestrians can be seen smoking cigarettes as they shop, quite unaware of the danger and the fact that the photographer is recording them all for us to see today.

A picture of a refurbishment in progress in the Grosvenor-Laing Building in Eastgate Street. From the 12th to the 18th centuries the road between Eastgate Street and The Newgate was known as Fleshmongers Lane. In 1965 it became Newgate Row which now contains the north entrance to the covered shopping precinct. The Grosvenor-Laing Building is on the site of Bollands Restaurant. Posters tell us that part of the refurbished ground floor is destined to house Boots Pure Drug Company Ltd. The gables of the building have been newly renovated. The original buildings next door were knocked down at the turn of the century. The Grosvenor Hotel is to be seen on the left of the picture and the dark coloured lorry in front of it belonged to Hamilton Bell of Halifax. A white-clad policeman directs the traffic.

At your leisure

For many years boating on the Dee has been one of the happiest experiences Chester has had to offer. The most beautiful part of the river is accessible from The Groves by rowing boat or motor launch. Two thousand years ago the 20th Roman Legion chose, as a site for its fortress, a low sandstone hill at the head of this estuary of the river and named it Deva. This was the beginnings of Chester, the date was about AD 70. The River Dee was once navigable all the way up to Chester but the silting-up process has been accelerated by the spread of *Spartina grass* which was carried over to British ports by ships which had picked them up in America.

A delightful view of Queen's Park Bridge, reminiscent of days gone by when the pace of life seemed rather slower and more relaxed than it does today. The first Queen's Park bridge opened in 1852 in order to link the new middle-class suburban development of Queen's Park, south of the river, with the town itself. It was designed by James Dredge of Bath. In 1923 a new bridge was built by David Rowell & Co. Ltd in a style regarded as more typical of half a century before. It had a span of 277 ft and its graceful lines met with widespread approval. Initially, Queen's Park was intended to be Chester's garden suburb, but the concept failed to take off. The plans were laid out by Thomas Harrison in the 1850s but only a handful of the proposed large villas had been built by the turn of the century. More modern buildings grace the street now.

Below: A peaceful scene showing the River Dee and The Meadows from Grosvenor Rock. Grosvenor Park was given to the people of Chester by the 2nd Marquis of Chester. In the foreground of this picture, on the right, a sturdy support for the Grosvenor Bridge can be seen. The bridge was completed in 1833. The terrace on the south side of Grosvenor Park commands a fine view of the Dee. Benches provided on this stretch of the pathway enabled walkers to relax and enjoy the sun, the river and the ornamental gardens. The main entrance to the park was to be found on Grosvenor Park Road and there were gates on all sides of the facility.

In the lower part of the park the thirteenth century Shipgate from the city walls and an archway from the the site of St. Mary's Priory have been re-erected. 'The Meadows' can be seen in the background.

Above: A sense of peace and tranquillity is created by this picture of The Groves, Chester's riverside promenade. The embankment above the Dee has been a major tourist attraction for many years. The west end, towards Dee Bridge was laid out at the expense of Alderman Charles Brown, one of 'the' Browns of Chester, in the 1880s. Refreshment kiosks and an attractive late nineteenth century bandstand all add to the character of the area, as do the landing stage for small rowing and motor boats which have been hired from the location by generations of satisfied customers. The spot has also been a regular venue for many regattas and canoeing events over the years during the summer and autumn seasons. It may come as a surprise to many people to learn that the Corporation once set up a floating swimming bath here in the last century, replacing the public baths on the north west corner of the city wall. A serious flood in January 1898 carried off the facility and it ended up resting on top of the weir. Three years later saw the provision of a more conventional public bathing facility in Chester.

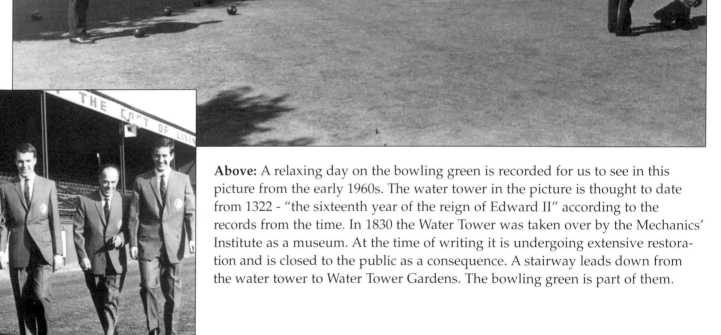

Below: Chester's professional soccer club was hovering around eighth position in the Fourth Division when this photograph was taken. The picture dates from February 1964 and features seven players and one director of the club in a photo-call designed to show off the new club suits. Pictured, striding confidently across the home ground are (left to right) Mssrs. Bades, Bennion, Evans, Butler, Starkey, Auckland (club director) and Flemming.

Above: A relaxing day on the bowling green is recorded for us to see in this picture from the early 1960s. The water tower in the picture is thought to date from 1322 - "the sixteenth year of the reign of Edward II" according to the records from the time. In 1830 the Water Tower was taken over by the Mechanics' Institute as a museum. At the time of writing it is undergoing extensive restoration and is closed to the public as a consequence. A stairway leads down from the water tower to Water Tower Gardens. The bowling green is part of them.

"THE 1960S PROVED A DIFFICULT TIME FOR CINEMAS THROUGHOUT BRITAIN."

Below: This picture of the Regal Cinema (ABC), on the corner of Foregate Street and Love Street, was taken in June 1966. Fifteen cars were parked outside so it seems to have been well patronised. The film being shown starred Natalie Wood and Daisy Glover. The architect, the same one as for the Odeon, was Harry Weedon. Up to the late 19th century this was a very built-up area with courtyards crowded with small houses. The Morris 1100 approaching the camera will bring back memories for many 1960s motorists. It was a vehicle ahead of its time, with Hydrolastic suspension which gave it a ride quality unsurpassed in vehicles of a similar size, though the rather wallowing get-aways associated with it were not to everyone's taste. The cars were roomy, nippy and quiet, and in *Vanden Plas, Riley and M.G* form - luxurious too.

Above: Chester's Odeon Cinema is featured in this 1960s photograph. The *'sixties* proved a difficult time for cinema organisations throughout Britain. The growth of television audiences and continued improvements in the quality of the programmes being shown resulted in a decline in cinema audiences. Many fine old picture houses closed or found new uses as bingo halls or furniture showrooms. Thankfully the Odeon survived and escaped the ignominy that befell similar establishments elsewhere. The building dates back to 1936 and features distinctive fluted brickwork - a hallmark of organisation's chief architect of the day, Harry Weedon. In more recent times the Odeon has undergone some extensive internal re-organisation to make it into three cinemas. It has since been re-named the Odeon Film Centre.

One of the finest zoos in the country, Chester Zoo celebrated the opening of the new Monkey House on September 7th 1963. The zoo, which has drawn millions of people to the Chester area over the years, was founded in the 1930s by Mr G.S Mottershead who purchased the extensive site. One of the many proud boasts of the zoo is that it only closes on Christmas Day. The zoo has functioned as a research centre to the benefit of the animal world, not just as a place of amusement and recreation for tourists. Many of the animals are kept in paddocks rather than cages, and the extensive landscaped gardens add to the many reasons for visiting this prime attraction. One of the proudest moments for the staff at the zoo was the birth of a baby elephant in 1977 - the first to be bred in captivity in the UK.

At the shops

Left: A picture taken in 1953 of Lowe and Sons who dealt in gold, antique silver and Sheffield plate. To celebrate the Coronation of Queen Elizabeth II they sported window boxes of red, white and blue flowers. A large Union Jack flies between the upper windows and smaller flags are tucked behind wall shields decorated with more Union Jacks.

Below: A good example of one of the distinctive shops which has taken on a modern appearance, while retaining the 'Rows' characteristic of being 'half above and half below' the level of the street. The picture dates from the 1960s and features the Travers ladies fashion shop. An illuminated sign just above the door informed prospective customers that 'young outsizes' were catered for by the garments of *Norman Linton.*

A busy day in Chester in the Eastgate Street area of the city, in a photograph from 1948. Many subtle features from the day combine to project an atmosphere of nostalgia, not least of which being the ornate street lamp on the right of the picture. Maypole Dairies -they had outlets in towns throughout the region - can be see on the left of the picture, alongside the premises of H.F Thomas and the National Westminster (formerly Parr's) Bank. The bank manages to blend in well with the contrasting 'black and white' architecture of the surrounding properties. It was built in 1860 and is known for the large Corinthian Columns which dominate the facade. Also in view is the Tamil Cafe, lower down the street, and Woolworths, each located just a few yards away from the Eastgate of the city.

A mixture of cycles and 1940s saloon cars gather along Eastgate in this 1951 photograph. Several old business names are shown in the picture, including The Fifty Shilling Tailors, yet another tailoring outfit with scores of branches throughout the country. The Pearl Assurance offices are seen at first floor level above the tailors shop and Richard Jones and Company the drapers had the shop next door.

Eastgate Street in a picture taken from on the Eastgate itself. The scene dates from 1956 and is interesting not least for the variety of motor vehicles shown from that period. The Grosvenor Hotel is shown on the left of the picture (just!) and the premises of Moss Bros., Woolworths and the National Westminster Bank on the right hand side of the street. More mature readers may remember the distinctive Kardomah delivery van, pictured at the bottom right of the photograph. A double decker bus is pulling on to Eastgate Street mid-way up the photograph, complete with large advertisement urging us to 'Try another Capstan.' When this picture was taken Britain was in the middle of the Suez Crisis. The RAF bombed Suez in November 1956 and feelings ran high in Britain with many street demonstrations and arrests. Brighter news was the televised wedding of Grace Kelly and Prince Rainier III in April, and marriage of the actress and sex-symbol Marilyn Monroe to the playwright Arthur Miller on June 29th.

A family business with something for everyone

The present managing director of Bookland is Mr R J Elsley but the business was set up in 1933 by his grandparents. Their first shop was in Liverpool and later a shop was opened at 19, Bridge Street, Chester.

It was very dilapidated and had a cobbled floor and opened in the depths of the Depression. However, Mr Elsley senior felt that things would improve and

that learning was important. Improved education was producing a public that was interested in books and reading.

The shop also had a lending library and flourished to the extent that other branches were opened in Wallasey, Bangor, Colwyn Bay and Ellesmere Port. A second Chester shop was opened in the new Odeon building before the war. Mrs Elsley combined bringing up her family with doing the accounts, buying the stationery and dealing with staff matters.

In 1945, after an apprenticeship with another bookseller, Mr J B Elsley joined the business and managed the Odeon building shop.

After the war there was a hunger for learning. The library and school supply work steadily increased and Mr Elsley senior often travelled to London to search out stock. In 1950, Mr J B Elsley and his sister started the Stafford shop and other businesses followed in Wolverhampton, Bangor and Newcastle.

In the sixties, 19, Bridge Street had to close. Number 12 was bought instead but as it was leased to other tenants it could not be used as a bookshop until 1978. However, a branch at 7, Newgate Row opened in 1966.

In the sixties business blossomed as schools and libraries developed, further education increased and books became plentiful and attractive.

In 1981 the new Wrexham shop was opened and has now become established. Mrs Elsley died in 1960 and her husband in 1977. Then Mr J B Elsley ran the business helped by his wife and other members of the family. R J Elsley became managing director in 1994. Bookland opened its 16th branch in Nantwich this year.

Above: The Bridge Street shop's medieval crypt.
Left: Set in a delightful Tudor style building, the Chester premises of Bookland.

Busy fingers in Chester

When Beatrice Hutcheson's daughter, Gladys was stricken with polio she opened the Arts and Crafts Studio. Here Gladys worked and trained other girls in the crafts of leather work and needlework. It opened in 1924 in the Old Central Buildings in Pepper Street and by the late 1920s there was such a demand for the suede belts that Gladys fashioned out of leaf motif that she could hardly keep up the supply.

There was a move in 1928 to Northgate Street. Rooms were taken over what was later Halfords and ten girls were employed in tooling leather, making fashion accessories. As well as a workshop there was a room for display and sales, but as it had no window on to the street to catch the attention of passers-by, Beatrice decided on another move.

After taking advice, she took a lease on a shop premises in St Michael's Arcade in 1933. Trade here was difficult as the arcade was a dead end, but Beatrice managed to make a name for herself before most of

Above: The Arts & Crafts Studio toy department in 1953. All the toys in the window were British made! *Left:* Gladys Hutcheson with one of her exquisite costume dolls.

Shortly after the war, Beatrice's son Donald took what had been the Red Cross premises opposite the craft shop and opened a toy shop which in 1976 took over the shop next door to expand further. The basement model department is a Mecca for the collectors of model railways, diecast models, kits and the radio-control enthusiast.

Today the shops are run by Beatrice's grandchildren, Michael and Nicholas Hutcheson. An independent family business for over 70 years, still moving with the times, the toy shop now has the support of 'Youngsters' toy buying group (which has a turnover in excess of £100,000 000). This gives them access to a buying power that ensures low prices. Through careful selection from some 66,000 toys available, the shop can offer some 5,000 lines, all chosen for quality, safety and play value. They can also offer collectors' models that may well become the valuable heirlooms of the future.

The craft shop continues to be a major supplier of all forms of needlework from counted cross stitch to tapestry, with all the ancillary threads, canvas, ribbons and trimmings as well as still being a major outlet for the world-famous Hummel porcelain figures.

Above: Nick Hutcheson in the basement model Department. *Top left:* The main toy showroom in the 1960s. Mrs. Massey, manageress rearranges the tin plate toys that are so collectable today. Note the dinky toys on the right. *Left:* Donald Hutcheson, son of Beatrice who opened up the toy shop shortly after the Second World War.

the workroom girls were required for the War effort. In addition to their belts the firm made trimmings, beautiful leather goods, beaten brassware, hand-painted mirrors and fashion accessories.

After the war the shop brought in more varied goods for resale including fine lace, tableware, baskets and Hummel porcelain from Germany for which the shop is still a major outlet. Gladys continued with her needlework, making exquisite dolls in international costumes. The shop was renowned for these for 30 years. Working six days a week from her work room at home she turned out dozens a day.

A cornucopia of confectionery quality

The story of Weinholt's The Confectioners goes back over a century to the 1870s when Ferdinand Wienholdt opened a confectioners shop in Market Street, Manchester. He was an expert in danish pastry and reputedly invented the Vanilla Slice. His son, August was born in 1874 and inherited his father's love of bakery. August came to Chester in 1899 to train the staff in a high class confectionery business in Bridge Street called Cottles, later to become The Plane Tree and on the site of Burger King. He eventually opened his own business, The Premier Café in Cheadle, Cheshire.

The family name was changed by Ferdinand's grandson and John's grandfather, Carl from Wienholdt to Weinholt during the First World War while serving in the South Lancashire Regiment in an attempt to Anglicise the name. The love of good food was passed on through the generations. Carl went into business as a fish fryer after serving in the armed forces during World War One.

Carl's son, Frank Weinholt founded the present business in 1953 after studying at the bakery department of Denbighshire College, Wrexham, and then working for Uncle's Frank and George before opening a small bakery and shop in Handbridge, Chester, with his wife Irene and sister, Margaret, and this being the entire workforce. After a very modest beginning the business flourished and the existing property was soon outgrown and the premises on either side acquired, enabling the shop to be extended and the bakery to be transferred from a lean-to shed some yards down the street to a modern building at the rear of the shop.

Son John had shown a keen interest in the business from the very early age of eight and like most confectioner's

sons had to stand on a box of fat to reach the bakery table. Leaving school after obtaining O Levels, John studied at Hollins College in Manchester, winning the award for best student of six months scholarship for craft study in Switzerland. He joined the family firm in 1974 after gaining experience throughout Europe and was responsible for introducing bread and developing the use of chocolate in what was a confectionery only firm.

With John's involvement it became necessary to extend and a second shop was opened in 1976 at the Bache, Upton, Chester. This also enjoyed steady growth and has been a very successful addition. During this time daughter Ann, who had completed a full time course at Manchester Polytechnic obtaining a Diploma in Food Technology joined the Chocolate department at Upton.

1984 saw a giant step forward when the firm opened a city centre shop at Watergate Street. The only available shop which was suitable in the city at the time was far too large for just a cake shop, and Ann had the idea of opening a coffee lounge at the rear which she managed full time until 1992 and in which she now, having a young family, continues to

take an active interest. Following Watergate street coffee lounge's success, Upton's small bakery was converted into a second coffee lounge and all production was moved to the further extended original bakery at Handbridge. John was by this time running all the day to day management of the firm, and after he successfully opened a second city centre shop and coffee lounge in Northgate Street in 1992, was made senior partner the following year - 1993 - which was Weinholts of Chester's 40th anniversary.

With daughters, Karen, Jane and Ann all contributing their expertise at various times to the business, the family believes that the success the company has enjoyed is due to total family commitment and a very loyal and conscientious staff, some of whom have given a lifetime of service to the firm, which is unusual in this day and age. The quest for better quality, service to customers, and new ideas is and always has been continual and ongoing. Frank's association with, first the Richemont Club of Great Britain of which he was chairman and later president and then the British Confectioners Association - Chairman in 1986-1988 and currently President, have played a vital role in this and have been of immense value - as well as giving a great deal of pleasure and the friendship of many business colleagues both in UK and abroad. Now John is delighted to have recently been elected a Member of

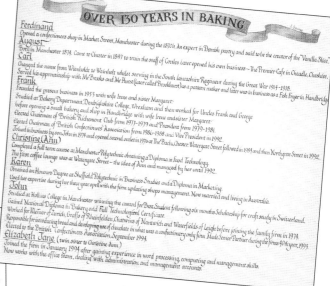

OVER 130 YEARS IN BAKING

Ferdinand
Opened a confectioners shop in Market Street, Manchester during the 1870's. An expert in Danish pastry and said to be the creator of the "Vanilla Slice."

August
Born in Manchester 1874. Came to Chester in 1897 to train the staff of Conlies. Later opened his own business – The Premier Café in Cheadle, Cheshire.

Carl
Changed the name from Wienholt to Weinholt whilst serving in the South Lancashire Regiment during the Great War 1914-1918. Served his apprenticeship with Mr Brooks and Mr Hurst (later called Brookhurst) as a pattern maker and later in business as a Fish Fryer in Handbridge.

Frank
Founded the present business in 1953 with wife Irene and sister Margaret. Studied at Bakery Department, Denbighshire College, Wrexham and then worked for Uncles Frank and George before opening a small bakery and shop in Handbridge with wife Irene and sister Margaret. Elected Chairman of British Richemont Club from 1977-1979 and President from 1979-1981. Elected Chairman of British Confectioners Association from 1986-1988 and Vice President in 1992. Joined in business by son John in 1974 and opened second outlet in 1970 at The Bach, Chester. Watergate Street followed in 1984 and then Northgate Street in 1992.

Christine (Ann)
Completed a full term course at Manchester Polytechnic obtaining a Diploma in Food Technology. The first coffee lounge was at Watergate Street – the idea of Ann and managed by her until 1992.

Karen
Obtained an Honours Degree at Sheffield Polytechnic in Business Studies and a Diploma in Marketing. Used her expertise during her three year spell with the firm updating shops management. Now married and living in Australia.

John
Studied at Hollins College in Manchester winning the award for Best Student following six months Scholarship for craft study in Switzerland. Gained National Diploma in Bakery and Full Technological Certificate. Worked for Rietner of Zurich, Graffs of Rheinfelden, Chatwins of Nantwich and Waterfields of Leigh before joining the family firm in 1974. Responsible for introducing bread and developing use of chocolate in what was a confectionery only firm. Made Senior Partner during the firms 40th year, 1993. Elected to the British Confectioners Association September 1994.

Elizabeth Jane (twin sister to Christine Ann)
Joined the firm in January 1994 after gaining experience in word processing, computing and management skills. Now works with the office team, dealing with administration and management accounts.

the British Confectioners Association and is looking forward to his association with them. Weinholts have been lucky enough to be involved in the making of some very 'Special' cakes over the years for Royal occasions and for Dukes and Lords.

This has often meant a lot of extra work but has given tremendous boost to family and staff alike; and has helped to make the day to day grind seen more worthwhile. At the moment the firm is in a period of consolidation following considerable expenditure with complete shop refits over the last five years and that largely during a period of world recession. What is clear is that any further retail outlet will surely necessitate a larger and even better equipped bakery.

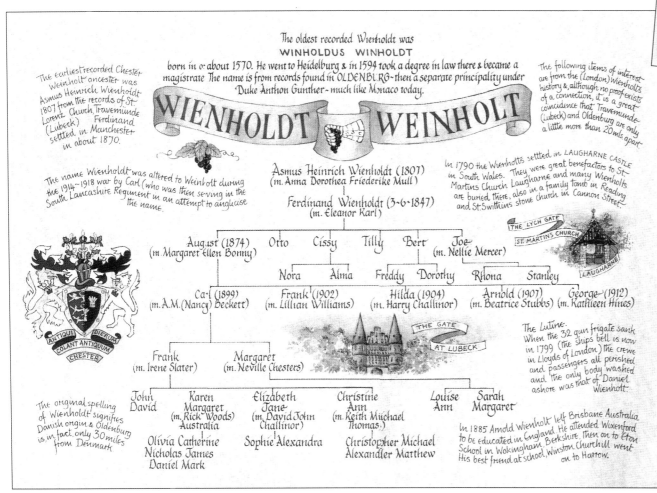

The earliest recorded Chester Weinholt ancestor was Asmus Heinrich Wienholdt from the records of St Lorenz Church, Travemünde (Lubeck) Ferdinand settled in Manchester in about 1870.

The oldest recorded Wierholdt was **WINHOLDUS WINHOLDT** born in or about 1570. He went to Heidelburg & in 1594 took a degree in law there & became a magistrate. The name is from records found in OLDENBURG – then a separate principality under Duke Anthon Gunther – much like Monaco today.

The following items of interest are from the (London) Weinholts history &, although no proof exists of a connection, it is a great coincidence that Travemunde (Lubeck) and Oldenburg are only a little more than 20 mls apart.

WIENHOLDT — WEINHOLT

The name Wienholt was altered to Weinholt during the 1914-1918 war by Carl (who was then serving in the South Lancashire Regiment in an attempt to anglicise the name.

Asmus Heinrich Wienholdt (1807) (m. Anna Dorothea Friederike Mull)

Ferdinand Wienholdt (3-6-1847) (m. Eleanor Karl)

In 1790 the Wienholts settled in LAUGHARNE CASTLE in South Wales. They were great benefactors to St Martins Church Laugharne and many Wienholts are buried there, also in a family tomb in Reading and St Swithins stone church in Cannon Street.

THE LYCH GATE — ST MARTINS CHURCH — LAUGHARNE

August (1874) (m. Margaret Ellen Bonny) — Otto — Cissy — Tilly — Bert — Joe (m. Nellie Mercer)

Nora — Alma — Freddy — Dorothy — Rhona — Stanley

Carl (1899) (m. A.M. (Nancy) Beckett) — Frank (1902) (m. Lillian Williams) — Hilda (1904) (m. Harry Challinor) — Arnold (1907) (m. Beatrice Stubbs) — George (1912) (m. Kathleen Hines)

The Lutine. When the 32 gun frigate sank in 1799 (the ships bell is now in Lloyds of London) the crewe and passengers all perished and the only body washed ashore was that of Daniel Wienholt.

THE GATE AT LUBECK

Frank (m. Irene Slater) — Margaret (m. Neville Chesters)

The original spelling of Wienholt signifies Danish origin & Oldenburg is in fact, only 30 miles from Denmark.

John David — Karen Margaret (m. Rick Woods) Australia — Elizabeth Jane (m. David John Challinor) — Christine Ann (m. Keith Michael Thomas) — Louise Ann — Sarah Margaret

Olivia Catherine Nicholas James Daniel Mark — Sophie Alexandra — Christopher Michael Alexander Matthew

In 1885 Arnold Wienholt left Brisbane Australia. He attended Wixenford to be educated in England. Then on to Eton School in Wokingham, Berkshire. Winston Churchill went on to Harrow. His best friend at school, Winston Churchill went on to Harrow.

ANTIQUI DIERUM COLANT ANTIQUUM CHESTER

Above and left: Two artist's impressions of the firm's 'family tree', the one above more family orientated and the one on the left based on the company.

Facing page: John's great grandfather, August Wienholt with his wife and staff of The Premier Café during the 1920s.

Typewriter Exchange - the company that offers Imperial service

Typewriter Exchange (Chester) Ltd was founded in the City of Chester in 1931 for the supply & servicing of Business Equipment to commercial companies throughout Cheshire & North Wales. The original founders of the company were William Cooper & Arnold Williams but the controlling share of the company was bought out in 1959 by William (Bill) Carter and the Carter family still today have an active interest in the business.

In 1932 Typewriter Exchange were appointed sole agents for the supply and servicing of Imperial typewriters in their area. This was quite an accolade as Imperial were then the most prominent British manufacturer of typewriters and remained so until the mid 1970's.

In the early days a major proportion of the activity of the company was involved with the repair and servicing of Imperial and other makes of manual and portable typewriters. Engineers would visit firms with whom the company had a contract. These included household names such as Rolls Royce Motors, BICC, British Steel, and all the High Street Banks. Between one and two hundred machines could be serviced on a visit with either individuals or teams of engineers and apprentices visiting the offices as appropriate.

Commercial vans, a motorcycle with sidecar and even public transport were used to transport the

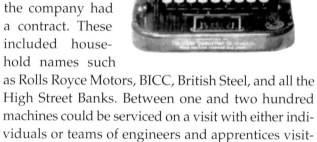

Above and right: *An Imperial Model 50 typewriter and the Oliver (Model 5) can still be seen at Typewriter Exchange.*
Left: *This building, which dates back to the 19th century, occupied the site of the existing premises which were built in the mid 1960s.*

personnel between Chester and places as far afield as Aberystwyth, Barmouth, Caernarvon and Anglesey.

Some machines were beyond onsite attention and had to be brought back to the workshop for overhaul. This involved stripping down the machine and submerging it in a bath of degreasing solution.

It was then dipped in a mixture of paraffin and oil for lubrication and rebuilt. The tools in use were simple. There was an air compressor to remove dust and debris and final adjustments were carried out with screw drivers, spanners and type aligning tools.

In those days the workshop was heated with a cast iron stove that burnt coke and in winter it could take up to three hours for the room to become warm, so the people sitting closest to it could become uncomfortably hot.

New machines were delivered in large wooden crates. Some had a continuous feed of carbon paper from a roll. In this way multiple copies were obtained but of course the carbon had a tendency to deposit itself on both the machines and the typists.

Typewriter Exchange was situated in various

premises in the city centre but will probably be best known for its occupation of 59, Bridge Street Row from the mid 1940s to mid 1970s.

In those days all equipment had to be off loaded and carried up at least one level to the Rows and then possibly a further two floors within the building. It was therefore realised that these premises were becoming increasingly impractical, and a move was imperative.

In 1975 the company decided to relocate to its present premises in New Crane Street to enable business development and add other office machines, furniture and stationery to the product lines on offer.

These premises had formally been occupied since the 1830's by John P Davies and Sons Limited which many people will remember as a marquee and tent manufacturer but which formally started its days as a ship's chandler and sail maker for the thriving Port of Chester in the early nineteenth century.

Change is all around us but when we recall the old manual typewriters that were used in offices years ago it is hard to believe that the secretaries of the day produced the work on these heavy and noisy machines.

The electric typewriter automated the process but it was the introduction of the electronic machine which was the beginning of the end for the typewriter as we knew it then. With

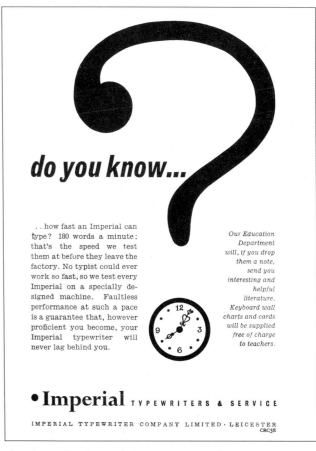

the introduction of the computer the typewriter is almost dead - but not quite!

Officewise at Typewriter Exchange looks forward to continued growth as Chester's leading one and only independent office equipment retailers.

INSTRUCTION BOOK

for the

Imperial 66

Imperial Typewriter Company Ltd.

LEICESTER and HULL, England.

Above: An advertisement that appeared in a typist's manual in 1953, claiming that the Imperial Typewriter could type 180 words a minute. Left: This booklet was issued by the company with its Imperial Typewriters in the 1960s. This model was the 'cream of the crop' at the time.

Five generations of quality family service

David W. Hughes Ltd's business at Guilden Sutton was the first frozen food centre where the customer actually walked into a giant freezer to do their shopping in sub-zero temperatures. Goods were stacked on shelves where customers could reach them without groping into the usual deep white chests in which frozen foods are usually sold.

This retail frozen food department of the business started as a butchers in Chester in 1885. It was set up by Edward Hughes who had previously been an engineer and his wife Emily, at 30, Upper Northgate Street. The business remained at these premises for seventy years. Meat and poultry were sold along with the family's home made sausages and black puddings. Whilst the business was still at these premises David Hughes took over control from his father.

Like any other, the business suffered some problems during the slump in the early thirties but recovered and opened another shop at 105, Boughton for David's son, David W. Hughes.

The family small holding at Mollington produced stock for the shops and in 1938 another farm was bought in Guilden Sutton.

There was extra work to be done during the war because of rationing. Contracting began at this period and Hughes held the contracts for supplying meat to the hospitals and for Chester and Cheshire school meals. Sadly, David Hughes died in 1942.

After the war the business expanded to such an extent that, in 1953 the Guilden Sutton buildings were too small. Work was done to convert them and an additional one was erected for meat preparation and packing.

Above: David Hughes, grandson of the founder outside the 105 Boughton premises in January 1936 with the very first refrigerated window display in Chester.
Far left: An attractive business card of 1938 which sums up everything the company produced.
Left: Son of the founder, David Hughes seen pictured here during the early 1930s. His son, also called David is at the wheel of the van.

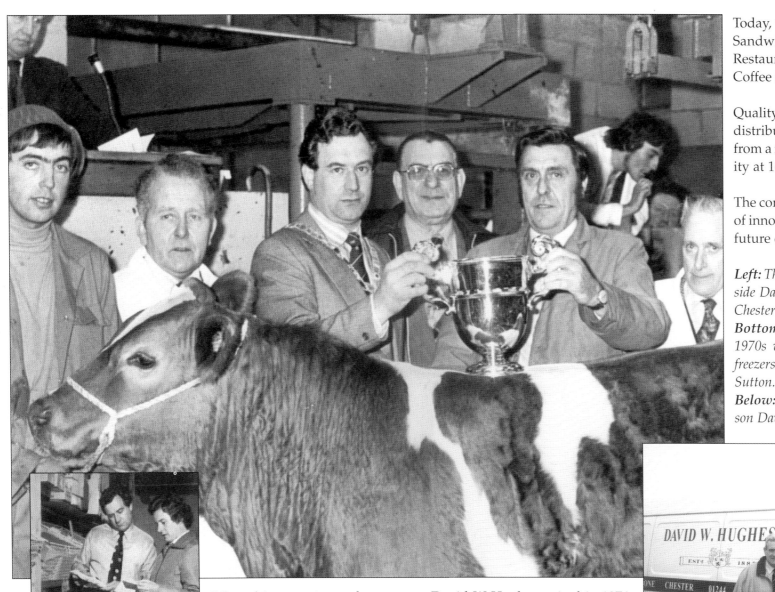

Today, the company's main customers are Sandwich Bars, Public Houses, Restaurants, Hotels, Nursing Homes and Coffee Shops.

Quality fresh meat and frozen foods are distributed throughout the North West from a new coldstore and production facility at 16, Knutsford Way, Chester.

The company's aim is to expand its supply of innovative products to both current and future customers.

Left: *Third from left is Peter W. Hughes alongside David W. Hughes purchasing the beef at Chester Christmas Fatstock Show in 1978.*
Bottom left: *Peter Hughes pictured in the 1970s with his wife, Tricia, in the sub-zero freezers of the company's premises in Guilden Sutton.*
Below: *Peter W. Hughes pictured in 1997 with son David at the wheel.*

When this extension and conversion was finished the shops in Chester were sold. By 1966 the business gained company status and became known as David W. Hughes Limited.

David W Hughes retired in 1976, leaving his son, Peter W Hughes in control. When Peter Hughes himself retired in 1996 it left yet another David W. Hughes at the helm.

Making beautiful memories for that 'Special Day' from The Bridal House of Chester

The Bridal House of Chester can justly claim to be one of the leading bridal retailers in the country - with a reputation which extends beyond our national boundary to the USA, Australia and Europe. This success has not been achieved overnight, for the business was established almost half a century ago, and has supplied well over 20,000 brides with beautiful gowns from top designers in this specialist field. Determination and sheer hard work have been the foundations on which the present company has been built. Success has been achieved through the determination of the proprietors, Stephanie Maltby and Gaynor Williams, to create delighted customers. A whole drawer full of 'thank you'

Above: Phyllis as a young woman. **Far right:** *An advertisement for The Bridal House of Chester. In its list of going-away outfits, it offers 'the very latest in synthetic furs, "Minquilla".* **Right:** *The premises before renovations took place.*

notes from brides and their mothers is a testament to their achievements and the high standards they and the salesteam have attained.

The Bridal House of Chester has simple origins dating back to 1952. The firm was established by Mrs. Phyllis Widdowson with the support of her husband Major E. W. Widdowson, in a stall in the old Chester market supplying ladies fashions. The business flourished to the extent where Mrs. Widdowson was able to set up a second *Phyllis of Chester* at 33 Lower Bridge Street. It was here, under the tutelage of Mrs. Widdowson, that her daughters, Stephanie and Gaynor, became involved in the business. In due course the focus switched to the highly specialised and exacting business of providing wedding dresses for the brides of Cheshire.

Continued success resulted in the decision to open a larger shop and premises were secured at 66-68 Northgate Street. Shortly before the opening it was

decided to provide the general public with a preview of the beautiful wedding gowns and outfits it would supply, by hosting a fashion show in Chester's historic town hall.

The show introduced the bright and vibrant colours of the sixties with dresses from *Ronald Joyce* and *Ellis Bridals*, firms the company still does business with today. The opening of the new shop was a day still fondly remembered by everyone associated with the store. Miss Chester 1968, Lynette Woolley, performed the tape-cutting ceremony which heralded the commencement of a new era in the company's development.

As the business established itself and grew through the 1970s and 1980s, the two daughters, now owners of the business following the retirement of Mrs. Widdowson in the late 1980s, embarked on an extensive programme of refurbishment. This provided a much-needed increase in the available floor space in the shop and revealed many of the Georgian build-

ing's secrets. From this time on, The Bridal House of Chester's tremendous range of stock could be carried on three floors. Visitors to the Northgate premises will be familiar with the layout of the shop; on the ground floor the area is devoted to mother of the bride outfits and hats. An impressive array of traditional bridal wear is on display on the first floor, including designs by Sassi Holford, Caroline Parkes, Suzanne Neville and Catherine Rayner ..... among others. Further bridal outfits are displayed on the third floor and alterations are carried out by the firm's dedicated and highly-skilled staff on the floor above. Virtually every item of clothing required by brides, their mothers and other female guests is available at The Bridal House of Chester, including evening wear, hats and shoes. All ages and types of ceremony are catered for with prices for wedding gowns ranging from £200 - £3000. After 30 years in the bridal business Gaynor Williams and Stephanie Maltby claim to be unshockable. "We have responded to requests for black wedding dresses, and red ones too - of all styles and lengths. We see our role as taking some of the pressure out of a day considered by many to be one of the most stressful occasions they have to encounter. People choose us because we have a reputation for helping them to enjoy their big day... its all about making them happy" they say. Every product on offer in the shop is carefully scrutinised to ensure the highest standards of quality, and it is this, combined with the most attentive service available anywhere, which has maintained Chester Bridal House's leading position in the bridal world. A consequence of this is the increasing number of ladies who selected their wedding gowns here in the past, and are now bringing their daughters to the shop to experience the same quality of service. "We pride ourselves on the attention we pay to every detail of our involvement in the wedding" said Mrs Williams "...but we insist that the bride takes responsibility for finding her own man!"

The **Bridal House** of Chester Limited
66-68 NORTHGATE STREET,
CHESTER CH1 2HT
Tel: 01244 340707
Fax: (01244) 311212

Above left: A wartime picture of Major E W Widdowson of Elizabeth Crescent, Queen's Park who died whilst enjoying a round of golf with friends at Curzon Park. Major Widdowson served with the Royal Engineers. After surviving the retreat from France he served in India and Ceylon before leaving the army with the rank of Major.
Left: The refurbished premises on Northgate Street, Chester.

The fascinating story of Edgar Maltby

It was in the dark days of post-war 1947 that Edgar Maltby set up his furniture business in a small shop on Brook Street which was, and still remains (though divided by the ring road) a bustling shopping centre.

Edgar had worked as a cabinet maker, for what is now known as the 'Stag' furniture company, and eventually decided that this was the time to go it alone. He had a dream which he turned into reality. Three generations on and the company he started is one of the best known and respected in the Chester area. He founded his reputation on quality, service and the ability to adapt to rapidly moving innovations as they developed, beginning with dining and bedroom suites finally expanding into cabinet furniture, carpets and upholstery.

In 1965, Edgar's son Maurice took over the running of the company. Trained and time-served in the furniture trade with Richard Jones (now part of Owen Owen) he was ideally suited to take control of what had rapidly grown into an expanding concern. Maurice soon bought the neighbouring premises and when 15 years ago Baker and Gale, the well known local butcher decided to close its doors, Maurice took over that building too, incorporating the premises into the largest retail furniture frontage in central Chester. A few years later when greengrocer Jacky Barlow retired, Maurice bought his shop also, this time to house the bedroom and rug showroom.

During this period, young Chris Maltby, grandson of the firm's founder expressed an interest in joining the company. Wisely Maurice insisted that Chris complete his A-level studies, following which he agreed to a year at 'Brintons' one of Britain's foremost carpet manufacturers based in Kidderminster - to learn at first hand the complete manufacturing process from fleece to finished carpet, leaving to undertake a business and finance course at Northampton College.

All that was in 1992, sadly two years later Maurice passed away. Now Chris together with his sister Anna run the company, but with the help of a team of hand-picked staff, headed by Diane Leech who operates the accounts department and her husband Mike - the company's carpet expert. Together they have notched-up almost 60 years of service with Maltbys.

Almost 50% of the company's business is involved in the selection, sale and fitting of carpets. Their client list ranging right across the living space spectrum, from small town houses and country cottages right through to some of Cheshire's best known stately homes. In addition they have carpeted the dining barges for the nearby Mill Hotel, 3,500 sq, ft. of working area for the TSB headquarters in Shrewsbury and even carpeted and furnished the complete residence for a senior executive of Shell Europe in Amsterdam. While here in Britain their clients come from as far afield as Northern Ireland, Scotland, South Wales and Southern England. Maltbys are, by the way, the sole stockists and suppliers of the world famous Laura Ashley carpets here in Chester.

Recently Chris Maltby decided to expand his already formidable display of furniture and furnishings to include an exciting, sophisticated range of lighting. Some Art Deco, some neo classical in design, including the very 'in' uplighting so reminiscent of the 20's and 30's yet currently enjoying an amazing 90's revival.

Although a relative youngster Chris Maltby preserves the same family principles that pertained when his grandfather set up in business - quality and value head the list with service second to none provided for good measure.

Below: The largest retail furniture frontage in central Chester.

On the move

Left: Foregate Street connects Eastgate Street with the Bars. A vast increase in motor traffic in the thirties and after the second world war made Chester notorious as a bottleneck. Traffic from the east and north-east, heading for Wales, met at Foregate Street and had to traverse the Cross, Bridge Street and Grosvenor Street to reach Grosvenor Bridge. By 1945 a project for an inner ring road was being discussed and the first work towards achieving it began in 1960. The need for it can be seen in this picture, taken in 1956. Pepper Street was widened and a dual carriageway was built from the Castle, through the north wall to St Martin's Gate to a new roundabout north of Northgate. The lorry in the foreground of the picture advertises Fairy, 'the mildest household soap.'

Below: A picture taken at the junction of Watergate Street with Eastgate Street taken in 1958. Two vehicles, foreground right, belonged to the RAF. The shops shown on the left of the picture were B Walton and Son, selling clocks and Beverleys, selling wines and spirits. The Cathedral can just be seen far right at the top of the picture. The photograph gives a good impression of the Rows on this section of the street, along with the congestion which characterised this part of town for so many years.

Browns of Chester can be seen on the left of this picture which was taken in the early 1950s. Eastgate Street, looking in the direction of the Cross is featured. The Browns store is seen occupying the premises at 34 - 40 Eastgate Row. Boots can be seen further along the road. The sight of the open-backed, double-decker bus is certain to rekindle fond memories in most people. The advert on the side of it was intended to promote Capstan cigarettes with the slogan "Have a Capstan, made to make friends." Motoring buffs will enjoy the sight of this old Morris 10/4 saloon. It probably dates from about 15 years before this picture was taken, but it appears to have a few years life left in it yet! We noticed the position of the electric horn on the 'badge bar' between the headlights of the charming little vehicle, but cannot think of the reason for it being there.

A major player in the Land Rover world

The history of James Edwards Chester Ltd, like so many successful business ventures, began in quite a humble way. During the early 1900s, two brothers James and Joe had a black-smiths shop at Lavister near Chester. There, they repaired agricultural machinery, motor cycles and motor cars for local people. When the car-owning population began to increase they moved to Chester and established a garage in Delamere Street in 1910. These premises had been used as a clothing factory with large adjoining stables. Joe Edwards' sons, George and Arthur, entered the business in 1920. George followed in his father's footsteps and became a mechanic whilst Arthur dealt with all the paperwork and the accounts. In the early twenties a mechanic was paid three guineas a week and was considered to have a top job with a high wage. At the end of the twenties James and Joe retired. They lived to see the start of the first agency acquired by the enterprising George and Arthur. The first agency was for Alvis but later came Fiat and Citroen.

Very soon the Edwards brothers had established their name in Chester and district and substantial fleet deals were arranged with Cheshire and Lancashire police forces for the supply of police cars and light commercial vehicles. After the war, in 1946 the Edwards brothers retired and the business was acquired by Mr Dennis Done, grandson of James Edwards. In 1948 Mr Done introduced the Standard Triumph franchise which he transferred from Anchor Motor Company which at the time held a share in the James Edwards business. In 1955 a further garage was acquired at Ledsham, named Two Mills. It was used mainly to prepare new and used vehicles. This was disposed of in 1957 and the

George Boyles garage at Mollington was transferred to new premises in Cambridge Road, Ellesmere Port where they were granted the Volvo franchise.

The Nissan franchise was added when the Company moved to purpose built premises in Rossmore Road, from garages in Heswall and Bebington. James Edwards then represented Austin Rover for the whole of mid Wirral in premises acquired from the Co-operative Society in 1976.

Since the mid 70s the Group has gone through a number of changes in ownership to reaching todays present situation as part of a major PLC Company. The Land Rover franchise has significantly grown to such an extent that it is now situated in state of the art premises on Sealand Road selling 1000 vehicles a year. However, what has not been lost with all these changes is the pride that the staff feel for its history and heritage and their dedication to customer service.

Above: The staff from the 1920s with James Edwards in the centre.

The company with a drive to succeed

spent so much time repairing the truck that he determined in the future always to buy new.

At first the new firm offered a general haulage service. He delivered Marley tiles, all hand loaded, and bought manure at five shillings a ton, selling it to Bees' nursery for fifteen shillings after forking it on and off his truck.

The headquarters to begin with was Rose Farm, Eddie's father's property. After their marriage, Eddie and Joan moved into a caravan parked in Bridge Trafford and ran the business from there. Eddie drove by day and maintained his vehicles in the evenings. Joan carried on working as a secretary for Crosville motor Co. Chester and did the paperwork for Farrall's at night.

After two years in the caravan the firm and the family moved to Church Road, Ashton in 1961. By that time they owned three vehicles, the Bedford O-type they had started with, a Seddon and a Thames Trader. The family had grown. Eddie and Joan had five children and two sons, Mike and Mark, joined the business when they came of age.

Eddie and Joan met with some difficulties along the way. The Suez crisis in November 1956 meant that all fuel was rationed. Joan had to run the office whilst bringing up the children. Later on, in 1986, a fire burnt out three units and six trailers.

The next move was to the firm's present site on the opposite side of the village in Ashton Lane.

Edwin C Farrall (Transport) Ltd. was established in October 1956 by Eddie himself and Elizabeth Joan Carr who one year later became his wife. Previously, Eddie had done farming work and lorry driving for an employer. Then he bought a second-hand truck and set up his own concern. He

Above: Eddie (left) and the first driver he employed taking a break outside the workshop.
Top right: The first fleet of trucks bought when the company moved to Church Road, Ashton.
Right: The founder and his wife at Rose Farm, Barrow.

These last premises, right next to Mike's home, were taken to obtain more storage space. They are close to the A54, six miles from Chester. They have an up-to-date workshop and 10,000 square feet of warehousing.

The firm tries always to employ local labour. There is an annual dinner for employees. On this occasion presentations are made to staff, an engraved tankard for ten years' service and a carriage clock for twenty. One third of the staff have clocks and three quarters of them have tankards, so Eddie is obviously an employer who inspires respect and loyalty.

In September 1993, Farrall Transport was awarded the BS5750, updated soon afterwards to the ISO 9002 which is presented to companies achieving an excellent standard of efficiency.

In the UK, work consists mainly of delivering to supermarkets, moving foodstuffs for manufacturers and transporting plastic granules.

The company has 24hr contact with all its drivers via a band three radio system and operates a Road-Tec System throughout. It stays

ahead of the competition with sensible grouping of loads, a personal service and ensuring deliveries are made on time.

Above: Burnt out trucks the morning after the 1986 fire.
Left: The first new vehicle after Eddie had vowed never to buy second-hand again.
Below: An aerial view of the workshop and warehouse in Ashton Lane and a selection of the fleet of trucks. Alongside is Mike Farrall's house and garden.

A picture dating from November 1964 which features the construction of the new flyover. It was taken from the direction of Canal Street. Traffic and the associated congestion and frustration it causes, has been a problem in Chester for many decades. As far back as 1945 plans were considered for the construction of an inner ring road which would help the problem by separating local traffic from the large volumes of 'through' traffic. Plans from the 1940s, in modified form at least, were realised in the 1960s and '70s. Many fine old buildings of character were cleared in order to make way for the inner ring road. It was a sacrifice which was said to be essential if the city was not to be completely stifled by motor traffic. Chester had been a notorious bottleneck in post war times and this escalated as the number of private cars on the roads rapidly increased. Conversely, the number of railway stations in Chester declined after the Second World War. By 1970 only the General Station remained after Northgate and Liverpool Road Stations closed.

The cellar of Northgate Brewery cellar is featured in this 1960s picture. Barrels are being filled from a vat in which the liquor was brewed. Interestingly there is a mixture of wooden and metal barrels here. The premises were located in Water Tower Street. They closed in 1969 and were demolished in 1971. The brewery site was shown, through careful excavation work, to have been part of a Roman rampart building, 'Intervallum' road and barracks. Also, cellars from fourteenth and fifteenth century houses were discovered here, along with the foundations of tions of later houses. The site now forms part of *Centurion House*, a section of which was opened in 1977 as the local branch of H.M Customs and Excise.

The company that has built upon its good reputation in Chester

After some years spent working as a joiner for a firm of ship-builders, William Richard Tilston decided in 1911 to set up his own boat-building and building contract business. His original premises were at Crane Wharf, where the firm stayed until 1928. Then there was a move to Dee Locks which is still its home today.

Throughout its 86-year history the firm has imported its timber from Sweden and Russia, Canada and the USA, Africa, the Far East and continental Europe. Its joinery work has prospered under the directorship of William himself, then his son William Joseph, followed by his grandson Christopher John and Christopher's son William Andrew.

The company survived the recession of the thirties with the help of a contract to build a new public house/hotel called the Peacock in Boughton. It still stands and displays the firm's handiwork today.

During the Second World War the company was seconded to war work making Lancaster escape hatches and instrument panels for aircraft.

Today it is mainly a service commercial industry, doing conservation work and maintenance of high quality workmanship in churches, banks and similar buildings where craftsmanship and high quality materials are the main criteria. Throughout the city, examples of the firm's careful workmanship can be seen and their reliability as craftsmen is respected much further afield.

Tilstons look forward to completing their century of trading, enjoying the continued respect of their customers.

Above: A coffee bar built by the company.
Left: The Old Meeting Room of the Honourable Incorporation of the King's Arms Kitchen in Chester. The picture on the far left is a very sensitive restoration of the room.

Deeside for a good deal

In 1935, Wilfred G John came to Chester from his native South Wales where he had worked in Newport as a joiner. Settling in Grange Road he began making wooden window surrounds for Williams and Williams, a company that produced steel windows.

The business did well until the Second World War broke out. It completely stopped production and Wilfred John was forced to leave the factory at Grange Road and have his machines put in storage in a local warehouse. For the duration of the war he made potato boxes, field gates and ammunition boxes.

When peace was declared, the business restarted

and in 1946 Wilfred took premises at Mickle Trafford, the site where the business still continues. In those days his raw material was round English soft-wood logs. In the nineties the company imports cut sizes from Canada, Sweden and the Baltic Regions.

In 1952, Wilfred's son, Grahame joined the company. It produced sawn and moulded timber, plywood, insulation and plaster boards, windows, doors and fencing. The third generation, David, is now an active member of the company.

The company moved with the times and their machines are able to produce timber mouldings in hardwood and softwood to any profile. These goods are supplied to builders and contractors, county councils, farmers and the general public. The

company has an enthusiastic sales staff and offers an efficient service at competitive prices from a comprehensive stock. Their plan for the future is to keep up the good work which is a philosophy that has led the company through turbulent times and will lead it into the millennium.

Left and far left: Deeside's distinctive livery ensures that the company is remembered.
Bottom left: The inside of the shop from the 1980s.
Below: The premises at Mickle Trafford where the company has been based since 1946.

Bodfari - the cream of the crop

The Pickering family has farmed at Rough Hill, Marlston-cum-Lache for over 300 years. The farm formed part of the Eaton Estate until 1920. Mr 'Den' Pickering built up an above average sized farm with a dairy herd, a pig enterprise and a flock of breeding ewes kept for fat lamb production.

His son, John, left school at 16 and soon after this in 1957 Den began delivering milk to hotels and cafes in Chester. The Grosvenor Hotel was one of the first customers. The milk was 'raw', straight from the cow.

Unpasteurised, it was delivered in metal gallon cans or glass bottles. Cartons were new and often leaked.

The business grew steadily with son David joining in 1967. It was decided to experiment with vending machines, cream and yoghurt and a milk delivery service was built up in Chester and Rhyl.

The rapid growth in sales of milk in non-returnable containers and the demand for skimmed milk brought the Pickering and Chantler milk businesses together in

> **"IN THE BEGINNING MILK WAS DELIVERED 'RAW' - STRAIGHT FROM THE COW!"**

1987. Soon the new company became major suppliers to four supermarkets. Then, in 1991, Northern Foods plc paid £28 million to occupy their position in the milk market.

Bodfari Ltd. is a re-incarnation of the business. After four years' rapid growth it processes cream to produce Anhydrous Milk Fat (AMF), a concentrated milk fat which is sold to food manufacturers, Walls, Mars and Nestle for example for use in confectionery and ice cream.

Meadow Foods Ltd. is a subsidiary company run by Norman Oldmeadow. It trades in a wide variety of dairy and food ingredients. The Pickering and Chantler families are major shareholders in the company and the 160 farmers supplying milk all have some shares too.

In the year ending 31st March 1997 Bodfari Ltd made a pre-tax profit of £2.8 million on sales of £125 million. It employs 75 people and is investing at least £1 million annually for new equipment and buildings.

Left: Dating from the winter of 1960, this picture shows one of the three Pickerings vans that made daily deliveries of milk produced and cartoned at Rough Hill, to milk vending machines in the Chester area.

Wielding the hammer in Bridge Street

The firm of Thomas C Adams was founded in 1886 by a Mr T S Adams who was born in 1856 at Iver Heath in Buckinghamshire, Mr T S Adams came to Holywell with his father in 1860. His father took up the position of Superintendent of Police there and young Thomas was sent to the then famous seminary known as 'Coles School'.

In 1870 Thomas Adams entered the service of the London and North Western Railway Company. He was ambitious by nature, and, after attaining the position of senior clerk in the goods department at Mold station he ventured into the Brewery and Wine Merchants business. Further ventures into mining and brickworking provided him with a great deal of experience which was later of use to him as an auctioneer and valuer.

In 1886 Mr Adams decided to start in business for himself and acquired premises in Chester Street, Mold. He built up a connection there that proved his ability in commercial life. Business came his way steadily over the next few years and in 1891 he wielded the hammer at one of the most important sales of property ever held in the town. The property belonged to the man who was to become General Owen Williams and it extended from Chester Street to High Street. In addition to conducting public sales Mr Adams acted as arbitrator throughout the country and helped to establish many important companies. He was consulted as an expert, gave evidence in cases and was complimented by the Lord Chief Justice on his method of valuing.

From 1876 Mr Adams was the friend and adviser of Mr John Howard of Sealand, the largest sheep farmer in England and Wales. He oversaw Mr Howard's property investment, particularly the purchase of the site on which was erected the National Provincial Bank and the old post office.

When Mr Howard died in 1901 all his affairs were left in the hands of Mr Adams who acted wisely on behalf of Mrs Howard and her family. When the Howards' immense farm was sold, the agents of the incoming tenant, Messrs Fox and Vergette of Peterborough, complimented Mr Adams on "the most successful (sale) they had ever attended."

In 1886 Mr Adams married an operatic artiste who sadly died in 1904. After Mr Adams' own death in 1931 the practice passed to his nephew, Mr T C Adams. After the latter's death the practice was sold into private hands and expanded into Chester and surrounding districts. The Chester city-centre office in Bridge Street was opened in 1968 and remains the largest privately-owned estate agents, surveyors and valuers in the area.

The present owner, Mr Neil Wilson joined the firm in 1970. He is an active principal with eight offices in Chester and the surrounding area.

Left: A bill poster dated 1938, advertising a Public Auction by Mr T. C. Adams.
Above: An early photograph of T. S. Adams' premises in Chester Street, Mold.

More than just 'messing about on the river'

The River Dee above the weir in Chester has for generations given the public great pleasure in boating, either on a day trip in one of the many large River Cruisers or enjoying the delights of spending a day on one of the small craft rowing up as far as Eccleston Ferry and Ironbridge.

The earliest public sailings on the Dee are recorded as being aboard large wooden barges, rowed by hired oarsmen, and these are believed to have been operated early in the nineteenth century. From these beginnings, a number of flourishing boat hire businesses developed with the original barges finally being towed by steamers.

The first steam powered vessel to sail on the river above the weir arrived in 1842 and was called 'The Albion of Chester'.

Of the many Boat Hire businesses which have operated on the Dee since before 1900, only two remain. Bithells Boats, which was established in about 1881 is the larger. The Bithells were a well

known Chester family and for generations had been fishermen on the River Dee and merchant seamen on Dee based vessels.

The venture into boat hire began with a partnership with a Mr Pollard in 1881, with one vessel named 'Gypsy'. Later in 1884 a new paddle wheel steamer (formerly a private yacht) newly named 'Dragonfly' arrived from the Thames and was put into service plying between the City of Chester and Farndom, captained by John Bithell.

After the death of Captain John Bithell, continuity of Bithell involvement in the business was assured by the family members running the business, incorporating four generations.

Two of Bithells boats were called up during World War II for service in 1940 and of course, the people of England had more important things on their minds than day trips on the river.

Business was naturally reduced at the time, although within a few years of the War ending, it

Above: The red-funnelled steamer 'Ormonde', named after one of the Duke of Westminster's horses. Picture a summer's day on the boat, with the music of the on-board orchestra in the background, supplemented by strawberries and cream at a local restaurant. Perfect!
Left: As well as larger vessels, the company also had many smaller row boats for a more intimate paddle on the water.

had escalated again. The nation needed a release from the years of darkness it had endured and boat trips had always been popular, never more so than then.

It was with some regret that in 1978 that a decision was taken by the family to sell the company. This was mainly due to the fact that the company had much competition from other leisure industries, package holidays to warmer climates were coming to the fore.

The business occupied a site of considerable commercial value because of its development potential. A civil engineering and property development company bought the assets which consisted of five large motor launches and over thirty rowing boats, along with the associated rights and landing stages. The boatyard site was only needed for redevelopment and later became the Old Orleans public house and restaurant.

As the developers had no desire to operate a boat business, they had intended to sell the launches in other parts of the country. However, at this point a Cheshire businessman, Bob Adamson, stepped in and agreed to purchase the passenger vessels along with all floating assets and rights. His action was the start of a new era for Bithells Boats, the name of 'Bithells' also being purchased from the original company.

There was a distinct lack of covered winter maintenance facilities for the wooden vessels in the area and it was decided that the course of action had to be the construction of new, larger vessels constructed with steel. In 1981, the first, 'Lady Diana' was launched, followed a few years later by 'Mark Twain'. The fleet now consists of three large passenger boats,

seating nearly 400 passengers and over forty rowing, paddle and self-drive motor boats.

In 1989, Bob Adamson was joined by Brian Clarke, previously manager of the company and the company became incorporated, each holding equal shares.

Nowadays, the company has retained its 'day-trip' appeal to local and foreign folks alike but has expanded its interests into corporate entertainment, wedding receptions, theme evening cruises i.e. Irish/Caribbean/Jazz/Disco. Times change, as do the people's ideas of leisure, but there is no doubt that 'messing about on the river' is as popular today, if not more so, than it was 100 years ago.

Above: The first suspension bridge linking Queen's Park with the Groves. It was built in 1851 and was replaced in April 1923 by the present bridge.
Left: The 'Bend-Or', which took turns with the 'Ormonde' to carry the orchestra.

John Woods Locksmiths - the key to success

This well known Chester Locksmith has been in business on Water gate Street for over ninety years. Founded in 1906 by John Woods, the premises were situated on land that had been occupied by locksmiths for over 400 years. John Woods established his business, knowing that it had to succeed, or else allow the shop to fall into the hands of another industry.

Success was almost instant. With an expertise that beat most of his competitors, Chester people began to turn to the infant company for their security needs. It proved worthy of its predecessors by thriving in an industry beset by cowboys.

Above: John Fieldstead demonstrates the traditional method of key cutting in the 1960s. John joined the firm in the early 1900s as a twelve year old apprentice, taking over in 1933.

Left: The original staff, with John Woods second from the right. The picture dates from the early 1920s.

John Fieldstead joined the firm as a twelve year old apprentice, learning the business from the ground up. By the time John Woods retired in 1933, John felt sufficiently experienced to make the older man an offer. It was an offer that was gladly received.

Since then, the company has remained in Fieldstead control, although it retained the original name.

Over the years the company has built up a superior expertise in its field, with its edge being the knowledge of the mechanics of a lock rather than just the ability to fit it. Capable of facing any situation head on, without pause has lead to a few moments of amusement.

John Fieldstead was once greeted by a man who carried into the shop a small safe. The man claimed the safe had not been opened for years and he was desperate to know its contents. Without the blink of an eye, out came the locksmith's tools and whilst the man looked on, the door was soon opened. The owner, his head clearly filled with visions of the untold wealth within, reached inside and pulled out....a pair of long-legged bloomers!

John Fieldstead retired in the 1960s after 56 years in the trade. His one wish for his retirement was for 'one more hour in bed every morning'. After more than fifty years of cycling to work every day, before the crack of dawn, it was very little to ask.

The business was passed on to his sons, John and Geoff and through them to his grandson, John, who now runs the company.

The shop distributes and travels as far as Manchester and mid-Wales, offering a wide array of locks and security equipment and its ability to provide the very best has led to a few momentous occasions, including the commission to make and fit a lock for the key that the Duke of Westminster used to open the bell tower at Chester Cathedral.

A company with generations of expertise at its fingertips, John Woods Locksmiths has a future that promises continued growth and prosperity, and with a fourth generation of Fieldsteads waiting in the wings, it will remain within the family.

Left: This charming picture dates from 1966 and shows the present owner, John Fieldstead on 'his first day at work'. John is the third generation of the family to run the business.

Montgomery Tomlinson - masters of soft furnishing

Montgomery Tomlinson of Chester is a company that designs and produces a wide range of soft furnishing fabrics and wallpapers. These are manufactured at their Bretton factory and the goods are combined in 'window-treatments' tailored to customers' exact requirements. Ready made curtains are also available.

That was not at all how it began. As present Chairman and Managing Director Grahame Tomlinson says, 1952 was a dreadful time to start a business. The one his parents set up in that year was a haberdashery. They lived in a rented house that their landlord refused to sell to them, so, for business purposes they took one-roomed premises in Upper

Northgate Street, Chester, opposite the Blue Coats School.

Arthur had previously been an area manager for Tootal Broadhurst Lee, the tie company but his wife, who had always wanted him to work for himself, encouraged and drove him on. They dealt in

Above: Montgomery's workroom in 1983 with the factory manager, Gill Bellis in the foreground.

Left: The present Managing Director, Grahame Tomlinson (right) with the founder of the company, his father, Arthur Tomlinson. Arthur began his business in 1952, in the middle of rationing.

made up early in the morning by his mother, the boys would climb into the back seat and the whole family would make the deliveries. John is now a doctor but Grahame figures largely in the rest of the story of the family business.

Monty and Tommy continued for two years in Upper Northgate Street where they acted as agents for Rufflette tapes and sold ladies' and men's underwear as well as wholesale furnishing fabrics. In 1954 there was a move to Falcon House, an ex-town house that had belonged to the Duke of Westminster's family. From it a secret passage way, now safely blocked up, led to the River Dee.

Left: Grahame Montgomery Tomlinson discusses curtaining with The Duke of Westminster in Brown's of Chester in the 1970s.
Below: Montgomery Tomlinson production manager with MP Peter Morrison at the opening of the new wing in 1983.

any kind of clothing or household goods that they could buy and then sell on at a profit, including plastic tablecloths and men's underwear.

Monty and Tommy, as they were affectionately known in Chester, between them managed every aspect of the business, selling, administration, packaging and delivery. During the week, Tommy would drive his old Armstrong-Siddeley all round North Wales, his old area for Tootals, picking up orders. On Saturday mornings they were grateful for help from their young sons, Grahame and John. Grahame has fond memories of parcelling up the orders, often for odd items and small amounts, then piling the parcels into the old car. After a lunch of sandwiches and the contents of Thermos flasks

London and cushions

When Grahame came out of the Army in 1957. It seemed to him that there was not much money to be made in his father's line of business and, in time-honoured fashion, he set off to London on his only means of transport, a scooter called Priscilla which he used for two years in the London area. It now has pride of place in the company premises.

He set up an agency selling furniture. This was achieved by the audacious act of driving 200 miles on Priscilla, interrupting a Board meeting of the furniture manufacturer in order to announce he was the man for the job of being their agent for the south. He duly got the job. In the course of his business, one day he walked into a furniture store in Holloway, in north London. The sofas and chairs looked particularly attractive and comfortable because of the cushions arranged on them. On asking about the cushions, Grahame learned that they had been made by the shop assistant's wife.

With Grahame, to think was to act. Before long he had met the lady concerned. She had been sewing her cushions in her council flat. Grahame took her and her husband into business with him, setting up a small factory. The cushions were popular and business flourished under the Montgomery Tomlinson name.

Taking his idea from a Canadian acquaintance, Grahame had the cushions made from fur fabric, a new fashion idea. They had a screw-button centre, enabling the cover to be removed for cleaning. Big stores such as John Lewis and Debenhams were customers and money poured in.

Grahame can recount many tales of his early years in London, such as pulling up outside the buying

Right: The Managing Director, Grahame Tomlinson in the late 1960s in central Chester.

offices of the leading department store on Priscilla. Whilst he was preparing himself, a chauffeur driven black Rover pulled up next to him with the Sanderson rep, who was also hoping to see the buyer. Both raced up the stairs to be first in line but Grahame won the race and got the business.

Back to Chester

Eventually there was so much business that Grahame decided to bring some of it back to Chester. He negotiated with the Duke of Westminster's estate to rent Falcon House at £6 a week for twenty years and part of the premises, an area at the back, was used for making cushions. Grahame had had his mother, Monty's help at the end of his time in London. She had worked extremely hard and learned all about cushions. When the business was brought to Chester Monty insisted on forming a separate company for it so that she had her own product and could make money for herself. She worked from five in the morning, often until eight at night, putting cut fabric into the car and delivering it to the seamstresses she employed. The next week she would call with more cut-outs and

pick up the finished work. She kept this up from 1958 until 1964.

The break with Grahame's partners in London had been amicable. After a while the London venture was sold and Grahame was glad to hear that his former associates had made a substantial sum of money.

By 1965 Grahame felt the need for a proper factory and a new one was acquired in Saltney. For a while business continued in both premises but in 1968 the company's lease on Falcon House was sold back to the Duke.

In the early sixties a textile designer, Michael Hadida worked out the 'Duplex' method of printing fabric on both sides. To Grahame Tomlinson, this idea seemed to have a future. Mistakes were made using too much colour, but the process was soon successfully refined and adopted by Montgomery Tomlinson.

And so to curtains

The cushion business waned but Grahame Tomlinson was happy to concentrate on furnishing fabrics, particularly for curtains. He made a trip to the United States of America where he picked up the idea of producing custom-made curtains. Going into Macey's he saw that none of the curtain stock was on show and that curtains were only made when the American housewives had chosen their fabrics and patterns.

In English shops, he realised, the workroom often took up a whole floor of the premises. He returned to this country and persuaded English department stores to put in his made to measure gallery concept in order to take order for curtains which he could make up in his factory in Chester.

However, English store managers were not enthusiastic at the idea of shop-within-shops. Dingles of Plymouth and Whittakers of Bolton were the first to take the plunge. The idea was a great success. Montgomery Tomlinson now has more than a hundred of these 'shop-in-shops' and Montgomery Tomlinson's flagship store in Chester is Browns.

The company's main markets are the large groups such as Debenhams, House of Fraser and other smaller specialist retailers. Abroad it sells yardage to EU countries, the Middle East and Australasia. Designs are produced under license in the USA and made to measure curtains are sold to Holland. To the ordinary household shopper, the firm aims to supply window treatments to all tastes for every room in the house. The company is now a market leader in made to measure and ready made curtains.

The company's plans for the future include a continued gradual expansion of its shop-in-shop operation and increased business with its existing own-bought accounts.

Since this time, it is important to note that Ron Prescott, who also lives in Chester has been a driving force in creating the design range which has enabled the company to be highly successful. Grahame has been ably assisted by fellow Directors, Phil Smith (Financial Director), Cliff Roberts (Operations Director) and Fraser Warburton (Factory General Manager).

Grahame is delighted that his son, Paul, who has his own business in Australia (Montgomery Fabrics (Aust) Pty. Ltd.), is now involved with the company in Chester. It is reassuring to know that the future of the company is to be maintained as a family business.

Left: Grahame's parents, Arthur and Agnes Tomlinson with his staff in the late 1970s. Below: A fine example of fabric and wallpaper designs in an interior.

Walker, Smith and Way - looking after the city's legal needs since 1831

In 1831 John Walker qualified as a solicitor. Subsequently he became Town Clerk, managing the City's business for part of the day and his private practice the rest. His junior partner, Sam Smith, whose strong flowing signature is still sometimes seen on old deeds, took over as Town Clerk and held the office until 1903 when J. H. Dickson, who had been articled with the firm became the first full time holder of the office.

The copier at that time was an old Remington needing a wet negative from which a print had to be taken when it was dry. A cashier sat on a high stool against a sloping desk in what is now the Reception area. His account books have been gladly accepted as of antiquarian value by the Town Hall. Copies of letters (even before carbon paper) were taken by the wet letter press method which left rather a smudgy purple ink on the original. The firm's first calculator was bought in 1958, costing £300, a staggering figure at the time and it was bigger than an old fashioned typewriter.

The senior partner's secretary, Miss Nayler, who started with the firm in 1915, was noted for buying an eye-catching new bonnet every Easter and the junior secretaries were very much in awe of her.

Above: Samuel Smith, one time junior partner of John Walker, seen here in 1890.
Right: One of the highly popular annual office trips. This one in 1951 visited Trentham Gardens. Miss Nayler, who began her career with the firm in 1915 and was famous for her eye-catching bonnets, can be seen third from the right, third row down.

The late Jack Blake is another legend in the firm. He knew the pedigree of most Cheshire farmers for three generations back. He served the firm for 46 years.

In 1956 there were four partners and about forty other staff. The great social event of the year was the Office Trip. The 1959 trip was to Blackpool. Faces were cheerful, though skirts were long. Rumour has it that two of the present partners had then only recently given up wearing short trousers.

With a history going back more than 150 years, the business has always striven after the qualities of ability, commitment and integrity. It has grown from within rather than by merging with other firms, which has allowed it to consolidate rather than compromise its qualities.

Many of the partners are 'home-grown', having been promoted from within. The policy of promoting staff on merit has led to high staff loyalty and long service.

There is a high ratio of partners to other fee-earners which is crucial to the way the firm works. All work is either directly undertaken by a partner or supervised by one.

Today the firm has 22 partners, about 150 staff and the very latest in computerised typing systems, e-mail (even fax is meeting competition), a clientele all over the north west and a high degree of expertise in many fields.

However, the basis of the modern streamlined service still rests on personal attention and integrity. The firm has grown entirely by its own endeavours and, with branches in Wrexham and Ellesmere Port as well, is proud to regard itself as the leading firm of its kind in the area.

Above: The 1955 trip was to Colwyn Bay. The gentleman on the left seems to be encouraging a camera-shy colleague. *Left:* A well-attended trip to Lytham St. Annes. This line-up of staff is arranged outside the Grand Hotel on Wednesday, October 4th 1961.

WALKER, SMITH & WAY
SOLICITORS

Dining in the traditional way

The impressive premises of Benson's Restaurant, allow patrons to feel that every meal there is a special occasion. The building began life as a fine Jacobean hall dating from about 1620. Known as Gamul house, it was the town house of a wealthy city merchant, Sir Francis Gamul. It is believed that King Charles 1st stayed here as Sir Francis's guest during the siege of Chester in 1645. The king is believed to have watched the Battle of Rowton from the city walls and Chester, the last Royalist stronghold against the forces of Oliver Cromwell, withstood a 20 weeks' siege before it surrendered.

Unfortunately, various subsequent private owners had little respect for the historical and architectural value of the house. A representative of the Gamul family sold it during the Restoration period and it was divided into small tenements. Later it was used for many purposes including storage, as an organ builder's workshop, antique showrooms and as an architect's studio.

Some owners and tenants made alterations that spoiled the house's basic design. For example, at one time the Great Hall was partitioned and a makeshift gallery was put up at the south end. Repairs were neglected and in 1972 the roof actually began to collapse.

In the previous decade interest had been growing in Chester's heritage of beautiful old buildings. Chester Civic Trust asked Dr John Tomlinson to oversee a photographic survey. When it was exhibited, the people of Chester began to realise the value of what was being lost. An Improvement Committee met, advised by the architect and historian,

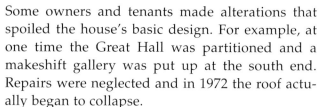

Right: *An early print of Gamul House. At ground level, where the lady in the bonnet and white collar is looking in, Bensons have built their bistro. The four tall windows on the floor above light the Great Hall which is now the main restaurant.* **Above:** *The current wine list offering a selection of fine wines from around the world.*

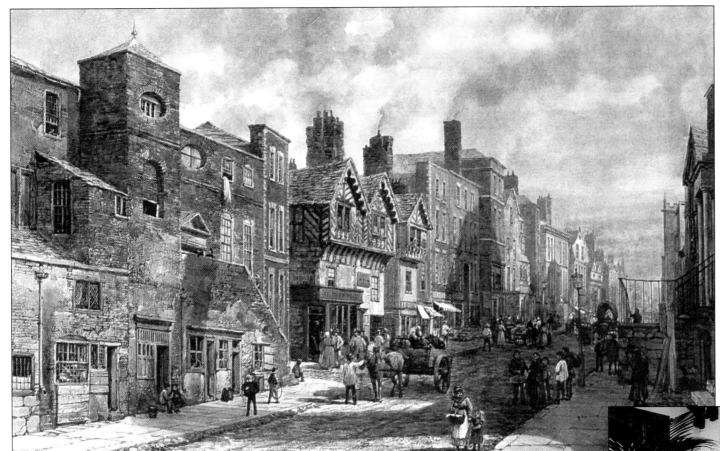

lease-holders named it The Frog and Peach, gave it pink toilets and decorated the wall with large green frogs. The present lessee, Mr Chris Murphy, has opened a more traditional English restaurant, Bensons, which takes its title from Mrs Murphy's maiden name. The main restaurant is in the original Great Hall. In 1996 the vaults below the Great Hall were completely refurbished, so that what is now Benson's Bistro has an exposed 14th century sandstone wall which has been renovated to its original form.

Right: A water colour by Louise Rayner of Lower Bridge Street looking north. Gamul House is on the left of the picture. The tower seen here no longer exists. The timber-framed public house with the herringbone bracing is the Old King's Head. *Below:* The beautiful interior of Benson's restaurant.

Alderman Philip Lawson. Afterwards a visit was made to Gamul House to see if it could be saved. Mr J H Chandler was of the opinion that it would be impossible to restore it to its original condition because not enough of the structure remained to indicate what that original condition might have been.

The restoration work that was decided upon cost the Chester council in the region of £40,000, the most expensive part being the reconstruction of the roof.

As the work progressed, further treasures were revealed:- 16th century stone-framed doors and windows that had been covered over and a window with its original diamond-leaded glazing beneath the plaster work.

When the work was finished the council offered the lease to suitable businesses who this time would have respect for their surroundings. It caught the fancy of several restaurateurs. For a while Gamul House was a Greek restaurant, then new

Education by Royal Command

On November 3rd 1877, a meeting of Chester dignitaries, amongst whom were the Bishop and the Dean, was held 'for the purpose of establishing a school for the education of the daughters of the Middle Classes'. Until that time, secondary education for girls in Chester had been available at the Convent School founded in 1854, and at a number of privately run 'ladies schools' within the city boundaries.

Before the end of the year, a lease had been taken out on number 100 Watergate Flags, a house built in 1779 on the site of an extra-mural Roman bath house. It was considered a suitable building for a new school, in spite of its reputation for being haunted.

On May Ist 1878, the Chester School for Girls was formally opened with an intake of sixteen pupils ranging from eight to sixteen years old. The first headmistress, Miss Constance Holdich, who initially undertook to run the school single-handed, sorted the girls into three classes. She was much impressed by the docility of Chester girls in comparison with London girls. Within six months, the number of students had risen to sixty, with fees of £10, £8 or £6, according to age.

In 1872, the city gaol, situated between the Royal Infirmary and Stanley Place, was closed, and the land it stood on purchased by the first Duke of Westminster, who then offered the land to the quickly expanding school for the erection of a new building. Designed by A. E. Ould of Newgate Street, the new school was constructed of red brick in the Tudor Gothic style.

Exactly one year after laying the foundation, the Duke of Westminster officially opened the school on March 7th 1883. At this point, it was still known as the Chester School for Girls, but after being approached by the Duke of Westminster, Queen Victoria commanded "that the school in question shall be styled the Queen's School".

Above: A very solemn looking picture from the turn of the century, depicting a class of teenage girls.
Top centre: A gymnastics lesson in the quadrangle.
Left: A 1882 line drawing of Ould's proposed new school. Queen Victoria's Statue was not included in the original architect's design.

As early as the 1880s boarders had been admitted, and were lodged in nearby houses, but in 1907, the boarders were moved to the north wing of the school, which continued in full use until 1941. It

was closed because of the risk of air raids during the Second World War, coupled with the need for more classrooms, and was never re-opened.

Although arrangements were made in October 1887 for the admission of a class of little girls, it was not until 1932 that number 7 Stanley Place was bought to provide separate accommodation for the preparatory department. The house was purchased with the help of Mrs. Phyllis Brown, a member of the family who founded "Browns of Chester", and vice-chairman of the Board of Governors.

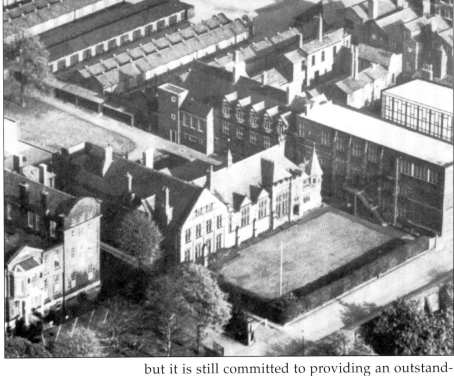

In 1946 number 57 Liverpool Road was bought, and in 1961 the adjoining property acquired. These attractive Victorian houses, now re-named after former headmistresses Mrs. Sandford and Miss Nedham, are where the present Lower School is based.

Following the 1944 Education Act, application was made to the Minister of Education for the school to become a direct grant grammar school. This status was maintained until 1976 when the phasing out of the system was begun, and the school became fully independent once again.

The Queen's School has undergone many changes since it was founded well over a hundred years ago, but it is still committed to providing an outstanding education for girls, and has acquired an enviable reputation for academic excellence.

Above: An aerial view of The Queen's School taken in 1961. This was shortly before the building of the Science block, which has been superimposed on this picture to show where it was to go.
Left: 100, Watergate Flags, the building at the junction of Watergate Street and City Walls Road in which the school was opened in 1878.
Top left: An open-air pageant from the 1950s. The School crest can be clearly seen in the background.

Applied education built on tradition: University College Chester

Founded by the Church of England in 1839 Chester College was opened by W.E Gladstone as the first purpose-built teacher training College in the country.

In the early days, the trainees would have worn distinctive uniforms, eaten with the lecturers in the refectory and would follow a strict code of conduct. It's difficult to believe now that two students were investigated for entering an inn in 1841. This was strictly forbidden for young aspiring school masters.

However in the spirit of this book which is about living memory, the post war years and, particularly the last twenty, have been revolutionary not least in terms of the appearance of the College. Passing through on the A540, you will see quite clearly a Victorian facade and a fine chapel but, on entry, the landscape reflects these changes in appearance. Bordered by three modes of transport, the Shropshire Union Canal, the railway and the Parkgate Road, the nucleus of the College has moved from the Victorian

Old College and Chapel towards the white brick buildings and enhanced sports facilities to the South of the campus. The reason for this change in physical profile was an influx of public money into the higher education sector and Chester's desire to diversify. From an institution with a high reputation for the training of teachers, the College moved towards a widening of its curriculum to reflect the needs of other employers and the local community. The archives tell us that the College's first intake in 1841 was 45 students. More significantly in 1989 (the 150th year there were 1100) and now there are 3,500 people studying on campus. The growth of the College has also meant a breathing of new life into historic buildings in Chester. Feathers Lane (opposite Owen Owens) for example had become a cause for concern for many local residents. Now the Victorian court buildings have been converted into student accommodation. The Grade One Listed Bluecoat School in Northgate Street, founded by the Bishop of Chester in 1717 has maintained its tradition of education through the habitation of the College's History Department who are now working with the Council's Heritage Services to improve access to local history and archaeology. Even the clock has been refurbished!

One aspect of College life has not changed. Even after this expansion, past and present students still talk of the "community atmosphere" and the "caring ethos." More recently this became more formalised

with the establishment of Student Guidance and Support Services but the mission to educate people for the real needs of society has not changed since College bells first chimed in the very first intake.

The College, now called University College Chester has a right to be nostalgic about its past. The tremendous turn out of the thriving post war reunion groups who frequent campus at weekends is clear testament to that. (The College Association has at least 5,000 active members aged from 21 to 1 01) But it is very much looking forward to building on its strengths.

Above: Chester Diocesan Training College, with Chapel and National School, from an early lithograph.
Left: The College has a long tradition of sporting success. This is the College football team of 1889. Can you spot any relatives?